In the same collection

The Louvre
The Musée d'Orsay
Egyptian Art
Picasso – Matisse
Modern Art
Contemporary Art
Paris

Cover:
Edgar Degas, *After the Bath, woman drying herself,* about 1895 (detail).

14 bis, rue Berbier du Mets – 75013 Paris

ISBN 2 86656 136 8

SELECTED WORKS

The Impressionists

Eric de Chassey

Translated by Anthony Roberts

EDITIONS SCALA

Contents

Collectors and collections

Although the earliest Impressionist paintings aroused the hostility of the public and the official art institutions, a few collectors were open-minded and shrewd enough to buy them in quantity. Largely thanks to these collectors, Impressionist works are now present in museums all over the world.

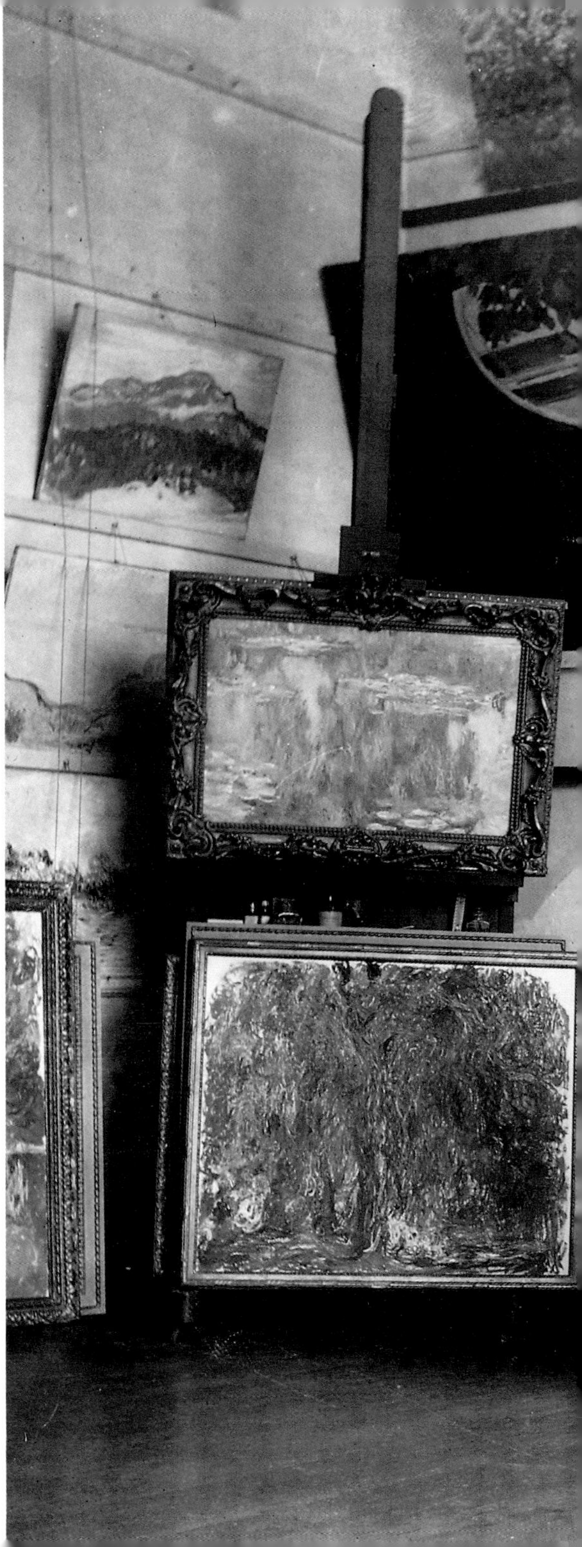

Claude Monet ▶
at Giverny,
with the Duc de Trévise.

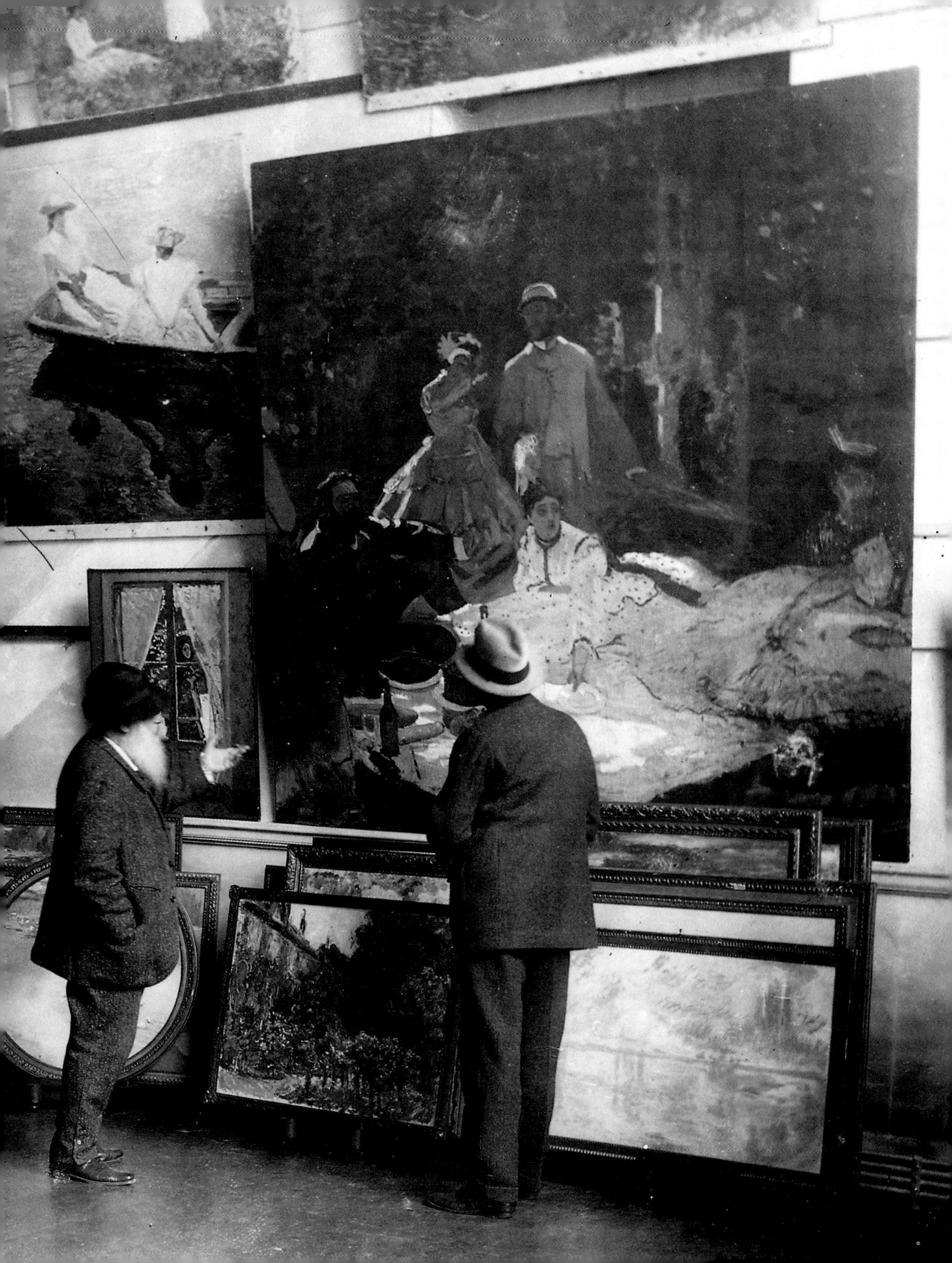

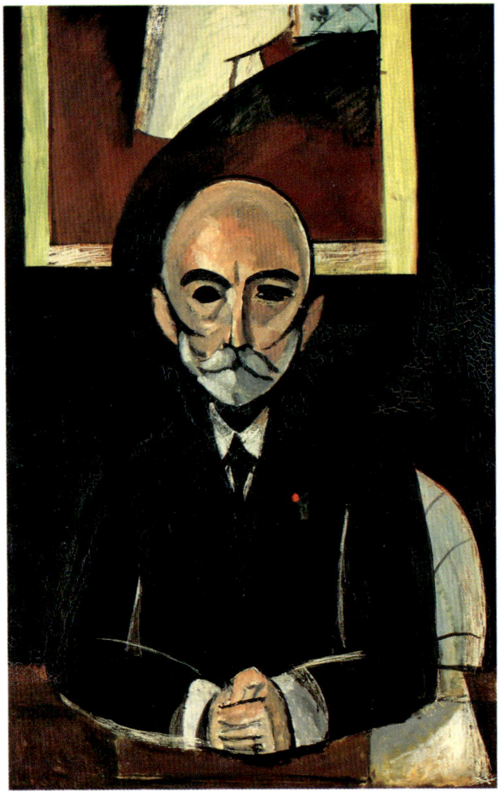

◀ *Portrait of Auguste Pellerin* by Henri Matisse (1917).

Pellerin, one of the foremost collectors of Impressionist paintings, is shown here with a freely-interpreted picture by Renoir.

Collectors and collections

When, in 1874, Parisians saw their first "impressionist" paintings at the "exhibition of the limited company of artists-painters, sculptors, engravers etc.", they reacted just as they had done since the beginning of the century whenever they were confronted by artistic novelty. They roared with laughter. Yet even by that early stage, the Impressionists had won over a few loyal supporters. In the 1850's, a generous art-lover from Le Havre, François Gaudibert, had made it possible for Monet to work in Paris, while Renoir could always count on selling his work to the Le Coeur family. By the 1860's the entrepreneur Ernest Hoschedé had built up a large collection of pictures by young painters, part of which was dispersed at auction in 1874, when works by Degas, Monet, Pissarro and Sisley were sold for reasonably good prices. After 1870, the art critic Théodore Duret steadily acquired paintings by Manet and Degas, along with landscapes by Monet and Sisley. These first buyers were usually people of average means: men like Eugène Murer, a restaurant owner who frequently accepted art in lieu of payment, or Jean-Baptiste Faure, a baritone at the Paris Opera. One remarkable figure among them was Victor Chocquet, a civil servant at the French Customs Office, who was a great lover of Delacroix, bought a number of paintings by Renoir and Manet, but above all gave special support to Cézanne, an artist who was almost unanimously rejected at the time because of his supposed lack of refinement. There were many other courageous collectors on the scene–individuals like Georges Charpentier, Doctor

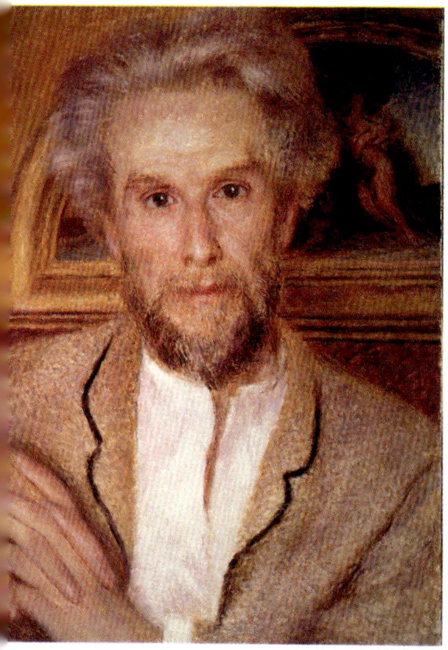

▲
Portrait of Victor Chocquet by Auguste Renoir (about 1876).

Gachet and the painters Bazille and Caillebotte–who took the risk of buying what nearly everybody else scorned. They were helped in this by the daring and flair of a small band of dealers, who in turn made it possible for the artists to live decently. Foremost among these was Paul Durand-Ruel, whom Monet and Pissarro had met in London in 1871. Later, when Impressionism's reputation was made, a new generation of dedicated collectors emerged, who included Etienne Moreau-Nélaton and Auguste Pellerin.

The art establishment took much longer to accept the new trend. Although the Musée du Luxembourg had been functioning since 1818 as a "museum of living artists", its administrators hesitated for many years before admitting Impressionist works. In 1890, a national subscription organised by Monet raised the 20,000 francs required to purchase Manet's *Olympia* for the state. In 1894, the French Republic would accept only a part of the legacy bequeathed to it by the painter and art-lover Caillebotte, which nonetheless brought such major paintings as Manet's *Balcony*, Pissarro's *Red Roofs* and Renoir's *Torso, Effect of Sunlight* into the national collection. In 1906, the Moreau-Nélaton collection was added to Caillebotte's, and was followed by a spate of purchases and gifts, mainly from the families of the

The Musée du Luxembourg, Paris, 1914. ▶
Photograph.

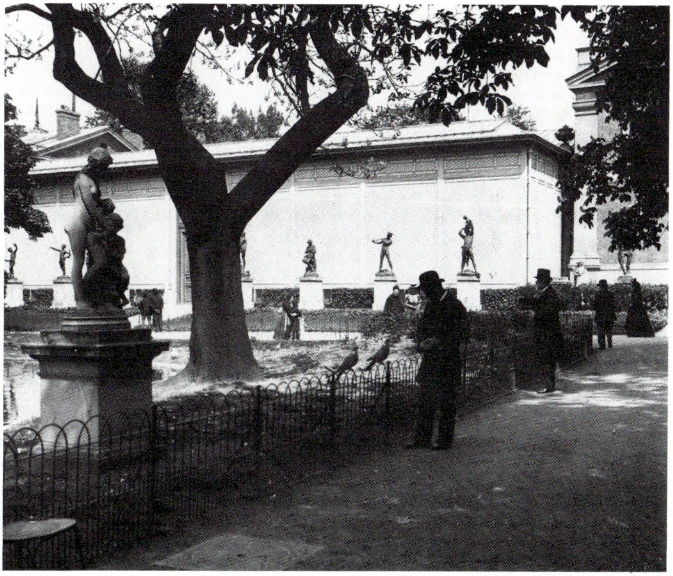

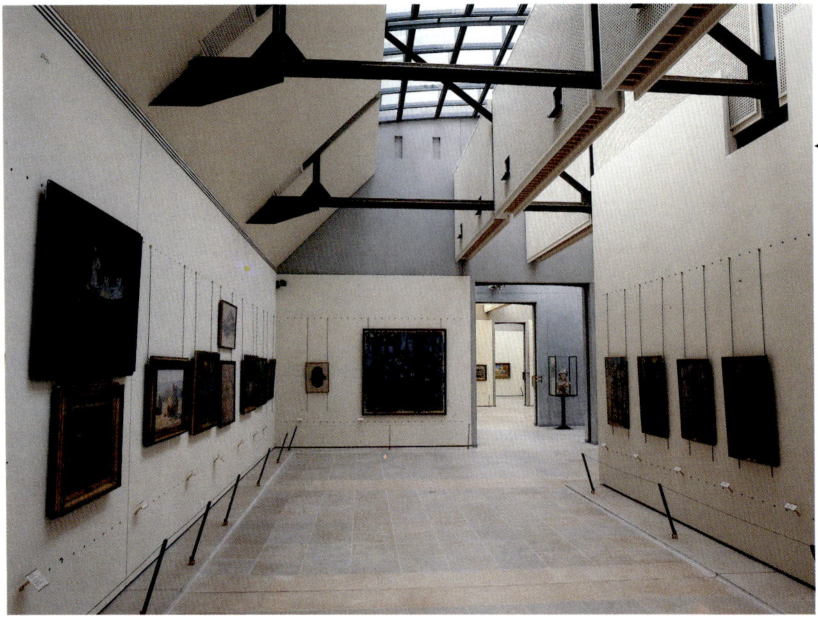

◀ Impressionist paintings room at the Musée d'Orsay, Paris.

artists concerned.
The public collection of Impressionists was transferred in 1945 to the Jeu de Paume Museum, and later (in 1986) to the Musée d'Orsay, which is devoted to 19th-century art. In the building which now contains all these collections, a former railway station converted by the architect Gae Aulenti, Impressionist works no longer have the pride of place they formerly enjoyed. Works done prior to 1870 are distributed around rooms in which visitors can also see pictures by more conventional, academic artists. Only the top floor is entirely assigned to later Impressionist and post-Impressionist paintings and sculptures.

Paris is rich in other institutions where Impressionist masterpieces can be viewed. The first of these was created by a decision of ex-premier Georges Clemenceau, whose popularity following the First World War was such that he succeeded in having the basement of the Orangerie in the Tuileries Gardens converted to house his friend Monet's great cycle of *Waterlilies*, which the artist wished to give to the nation. On the second floor of the same building, a major collection

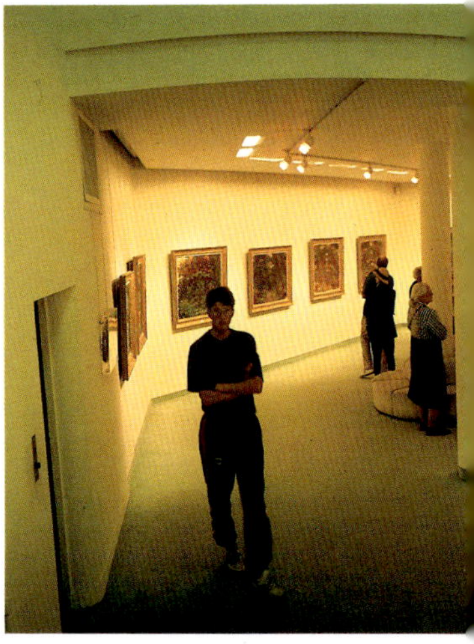

of Cézannes and Renoirs, collected after 1920 by the Paris dealer Paul Guillaume and his wife, has been on permanent display since it was donated in 1984.
In addition the Musée Marmottan possesses a remarkable series of Impressionist works, mostly from the legacies of Dr. Georges Bellio and Michel Monet, the painter's descendant. Finally, in the case of the Musée du Petit Palais, it was mainly the artists themselves, or their dealers, who donated major works to the city of Paris for this gallery.

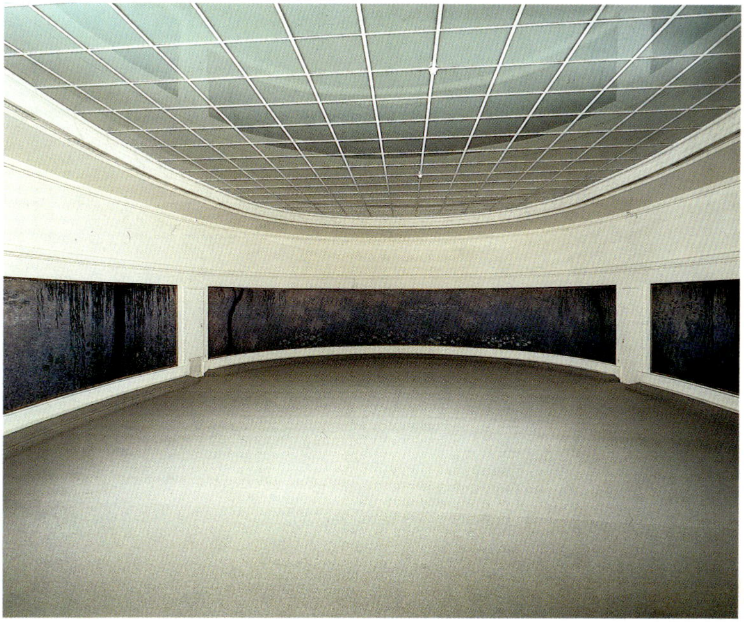

▲
Waterlilies room
at the Musée de l'Orangerie, Paris.

Impressionist paintings room
at the Musée Marmottan, Paris.
Photograph, 1994.
▼

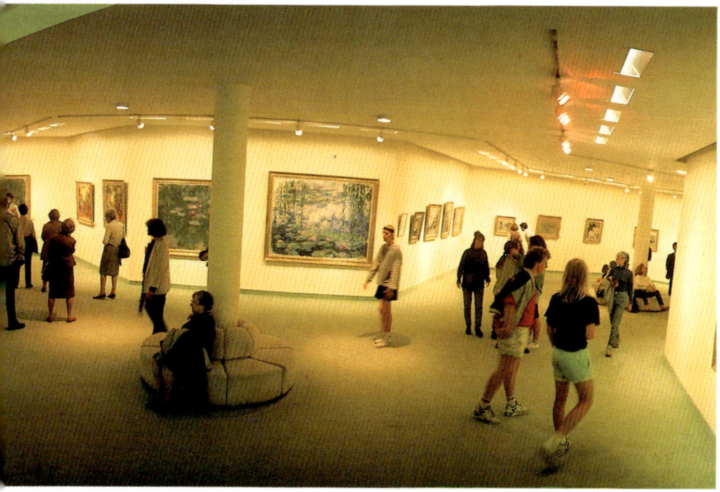

In sum, Paris today remains the undisputed capital of Impressionism.
Outside the capital, one can visit the other localities where these artists lived and worked; the Pissarro Museum in Pontoise, Monet's Garden at Giverny, Renoir's house at Cagnes and Cézanne's studio at Les Lauves near Aix are examples.

Impressionism was quickly accepted outside France, especially in the USA. Durand-Ruel's exhibition in New York in 1886 almost instantaneously created a reserve of American

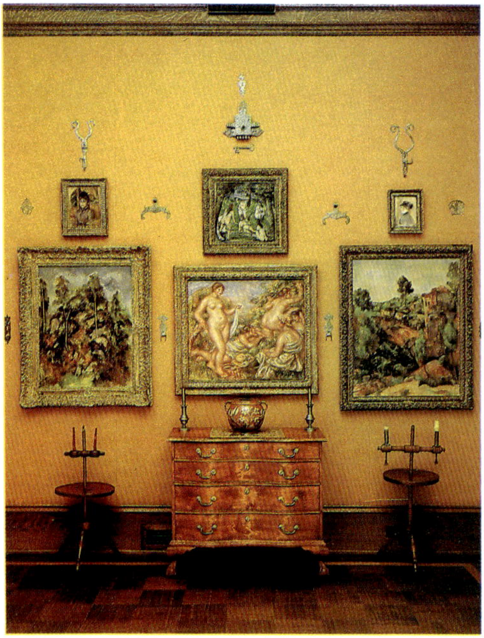

◄ A gallery at the Barnes Foundation, Merion, Philadelphia. The Renoir wall. Photograph.

Barnes bought Renoirs and Cézannes by dozen and hung them on the walls of his house as if they were elements of a single giant composition.

collectors, notably Harry and Louisine Havemeyer, who took the advice of their compatriot Mary Cassatt in assembling an extraordinary collection, later donated to New York's Metropolitan Museum. Moreover, the efforts of other private collectors made it possible for the Museum of Fine Arts in Boston and the Chicago Art Institute to accumulate two of the world's greatest Impressionist collections. And it was another American, Dr Albert Barnes, who from the 1920's onward pieced together the world's largest concentration of works by Renoir and Cézanne, now exhibited at the Barnes Foundation in Merion, near Philadelphia.

In other parts of the world, the reaction began more slowly, but when it did it was irresistible. In England, substantial Impressionist collections began to be assembled around 1900: notably those of Hugh Lane (which was donated to the National Gallery) and Samuel Courtauld, the founder of the Courtauld Institute. In Russia, in a few years at the turn of the century, two magnificent collections of Impressionist works were compiled by the wealthy dealers Sergei Schtchoukin and Ivan Morosov. Today these are shared between the Pushkin Museum in Moscow and the Hermitage in St Petersburg. In post-war Japan, where this refined form of art in many ways resembles the national style, there has been a steady growth of interest in the works of the French Impressionists ever since the economic boom of the 1960's gave Japanese collectors and institutions the means to acquire them. Indeed in modern times the paintings of the Impressionist group are ranked among the most important and valuable works of art on the planet; so precious are they that most are now in museums and public galleries.

Very few remain in the hands of private collectors and when these appear on the International market they are subject of intense speculation and bidding. As to the works assembled by the world's museums–and notably by the museums of

Paris, which in terms of quality, numbers and longevity have always possessed the lion's share–they inspire an admiration which their authors cannot have imagined, even in their wildest dreams, one hundred years ago.

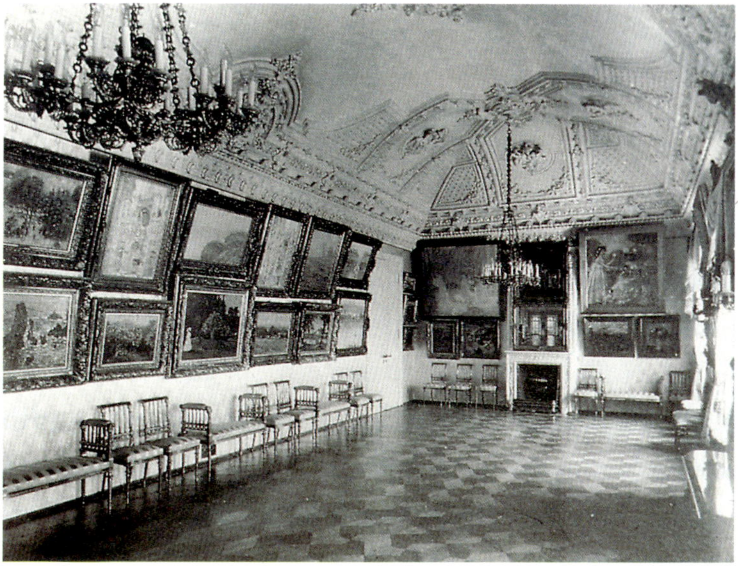

▲
Music room, Schtchoukin Palace, Moscow. Photograph.
For Schtchoukin, Monet's work was the very essence of Impressionism. Between 1898 and 1904 he bought twelve of Monet's paintings, which he hung on a single wall.

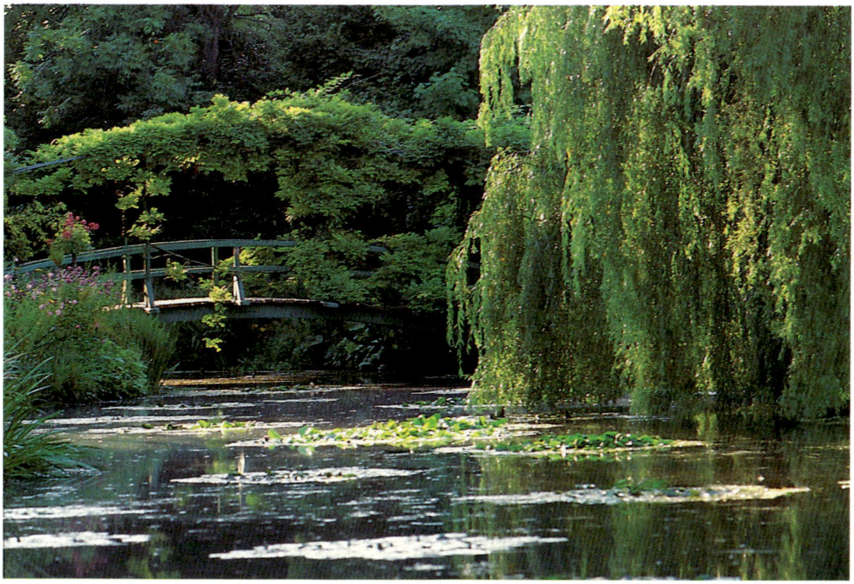

◄ The Garden at Giverny. Photograph, 1992.

Frédéric Bazille ►
(1841-1870).
Bazille's studio, Rue de la Condamine
(1870).
Oil on canvas:
98 x 128 cm.
Musée d'Orsay, Paris.

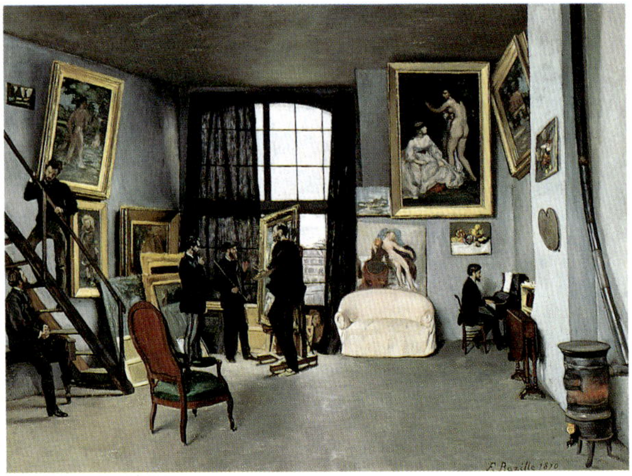

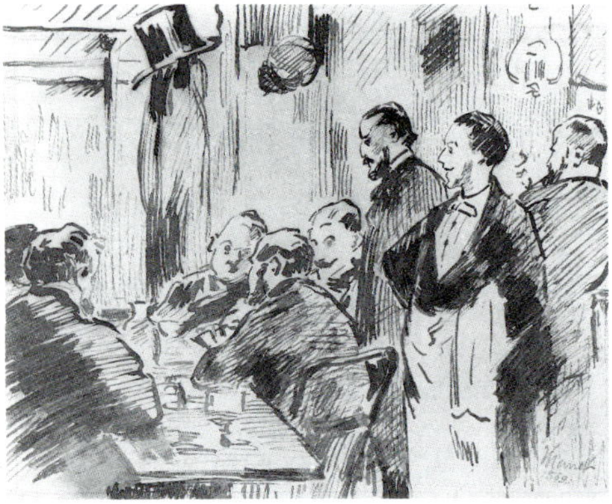

◄ **Edouard Manet**
(1832-1883).
Café Interior (Café Guerbois) (1869).
Pen on paper:
29.5 x 39.4 cm.
Fogg Art Museum
Cambridge, USA.

The Guerbois was a quiet café in the Batignolles quarter. In 1869 it became a meeting place for admirers of Manet.

Henri Fantin-Latour ►
(1836-1904).
The Batignolles Studio
(1870).
Oil on canvas:
204 x 273 cm.
Musée d'Orsay, Paris.

This canvas, painted in the classical manner, shows the young painters Renoir, Bazille and Monet gathered around Monet at his easel with the critics Astruc and Zola.

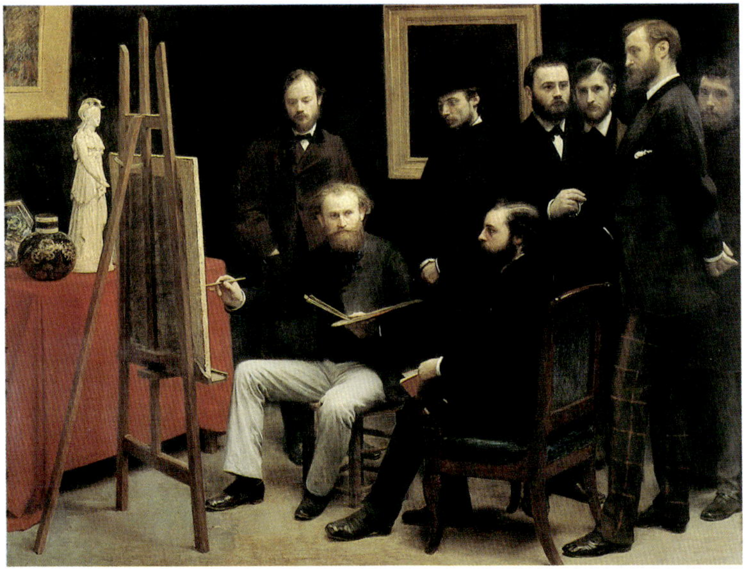

The impressionist group

When we speak of Impressionism, everyone knows roughly which artists we are referring to; the term implies a solid group of like-minded painters which appeared entirely spontaneously. The truth is very different, for it was only little by little that these men and women of different ages and social classes came together, by dint of friendship and mutual respect. They did so because they shared the same positions vis-à-vis the artistic institutions of their time. By contrast, their personal styles often remained poles apart.

The youngest of them–Frédéric Bazille, Claude Monet, Pierre-Auguste Renoir and Alfred Sisley–got to know each other between 1861 and 1864 at the studio of Gleyre, a longtime teacher at the Ecole des Beaux-Arts. From him they learned about classical perfection, transmitted by a form of teaching which had become rigidly academic. Above all they discovered that they had in common a deep interest in the direct representation of nature, and a horror of imitating past masters in the conventional manner. Before long they found themselves painting side by side, either in the Forest of Fontainebleau, or in each other's Parisian ateliers. At the same time they made friends with Camille Pissarro and Paul Cézanne, who had previously studied art at the Académie Suisse, and who shared their admiration for Gustave Courbet and Edouard Manet, two painters who refused to sacrifice their individuality to official constraints. At that time Courbet was spending too much time in his native Jura to build a strong Paris following, but Manet did not hesitate to surround himself with a motley group of friends, with whom he frequented cafés and studios. Thus it was Manet who became the dominant painter of his generation.

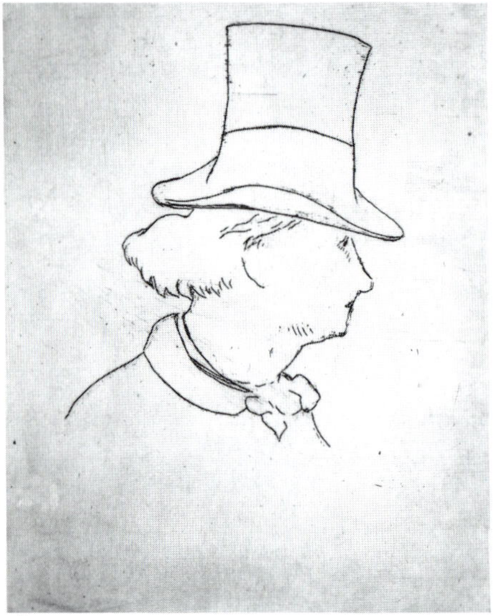

▲

Edouard Manet
Baudelaire, with hat, in profile
(1867-1868).
Etching, second plate:
10.9 x 9 cm.
Bibliothèque
Nationale, Paris.

Cham ►
The Impressionist painter.
Caricature from
Le Charivari
(1877).

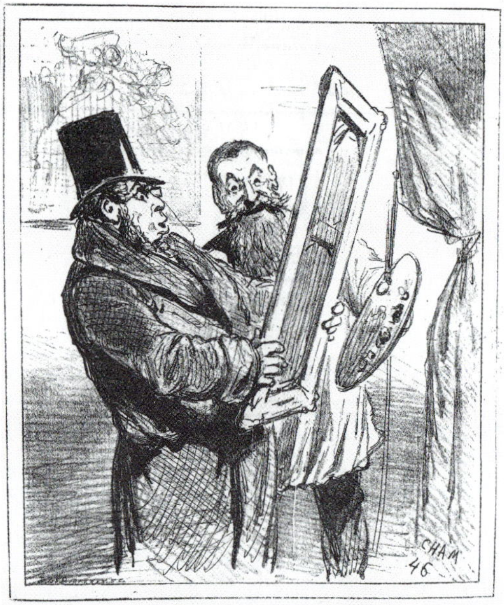

LE PEINTRE IMPRESSIONNISTE.
— Mais ce sont des tons de cadavres?
— Oui, malheureusement je ne peux pas arriver à l'odeur!

Edouard Manet ►
Olympia (1863).
Oil on canvas:
130 x 190 cm.
Musée d'Orsay, Paris.

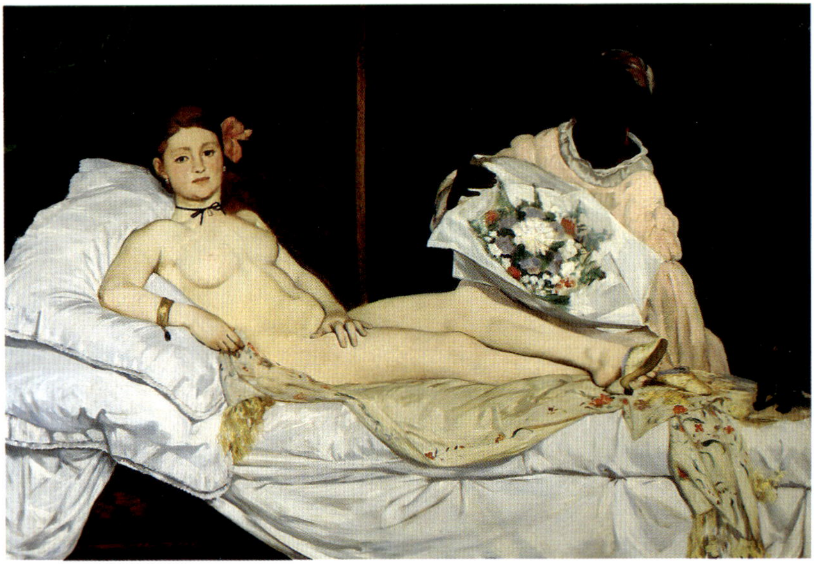

In mid-19th-century Paris, painters (despite their Bohemian way of life) were mainly concerned to produce paintings on highfalutin subjects aimed at the official "Salon", or exhibition, organized by the Institut. Although he himself was the most famous and respected of the academicians, Ingres had already described the Salon as a "shop full of paintings for sale, a bazaar in which the sheer quantity of objects has an effect of stupefaction, and in which industry reigns in place of art."

The choice of works for the Salon was assumed by a jury, which evaluated the technical abilities of the painters in question along with the suitability of their subject matter. At the 1863 Salon, the jury turned down so many works that Emperor Napoleon III decided to remedy the situation by organizing an exhibition of the rejected paintings. This "Salon des Refusés" ultimately attracted a wider public than the "Salon Officiel". Pictures which were thought badly painted were as usual roundly mocked, but the high point of the show was the scandal created by Edouard Manet's *Luncheon on the Grass (Déjeuner sur l'Herbe)*.

Manet had no desire to shock; he merely saw no reason to obey the narrow precepts of the Academy. In 1865, he succeeded in showing two paintings at the salon, a nude and a religious subject, whose juxtaposition provoked an even greater scandal: these were *Olympia* and *Jesus Taunted by the Soldiers*. Manet was heaped with abuse, even by the habitual defenders of Courbet, who reproached him with forgetting nature and painting "playing cards". His few supporters were his young painter friends and a small group of perceptive poets and writers like Charles Baudelaire.

Pierre-Auguste Renoir ►
(1841-1919).
Frédéric Bazille at his easel
(1867).
Oil on canvas:
105 x 75 cm.
Musée d'Orsay,
Paris.

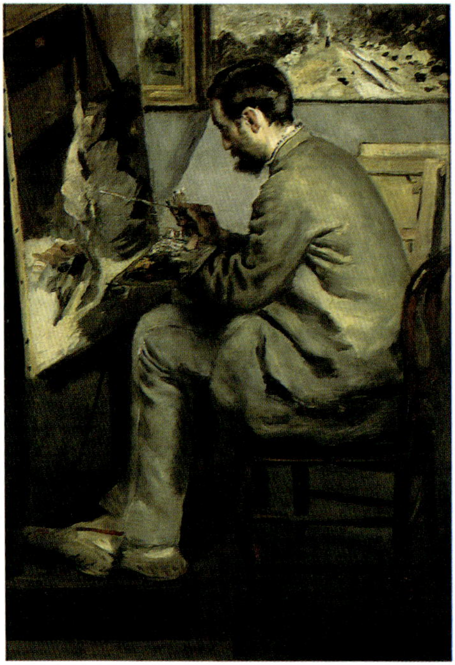

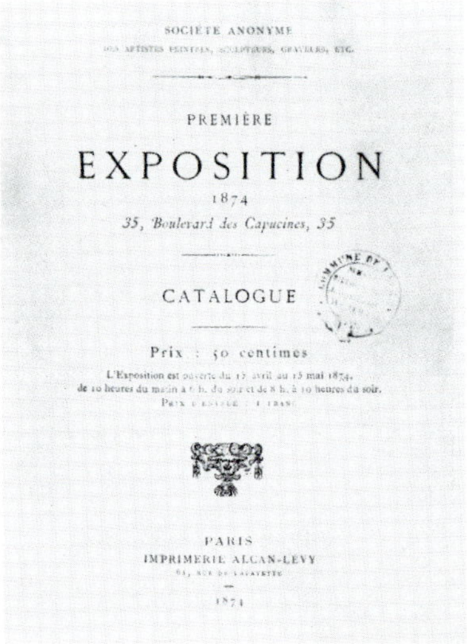

SOCIÉTÉ ANONYME
DES ARTISTES PEINTRES, SCULPTEURS, GRAVEURS, ETC.

PREMIÈRE

EXPOSITION

1874

35, Boulevard des Capucines, 35

CATALOGUE

Prix : 50 centimes

L'Exposition est ouverte du 15 avril au 15 mai 1874,
de 10 heures du matin à 6 h. du soir et de 8 h. à 10 heures du soir.
Prix d'entrée : 1 franc

PARIS
IMPRIMERIE ALCAN-LEVY
61, rue de Lafayette

1874

▲
Catalogue of the first Impressionist exhibition in Paris, April 15–May 15 1874.

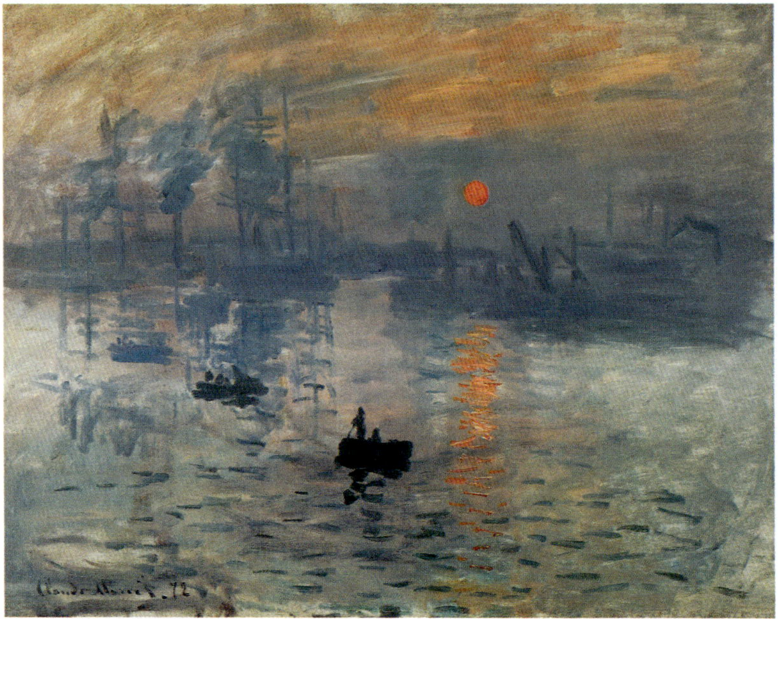

Claude Monet ►
(1840-1926).
Impression, Sunrise
(1874).
Oil on canvas:
48 x 63 cm.
Musée Marmottan,
Paris.

Manet refused to condemn the official art institutions: on the contrary, he did what he could to win their approval. But his friends began to take the view that they would have to exhibit their own paintings themselves, if they wanted them shown under favourable circumstances. As early as 1867, Monet was suggesting that they should organize an exhibition at their own expense.
The War of 1870 and the Commune uprising in Paris the next year made the old institutions irrelevant, and the time seemed ripe for something more daring in the realm of art. Manet had his first real success with the public at the Salon of 1873, when everyone agreed he had "at last seen sense". This success convinced Monet that his old project should be resurrected. Edgar Degas and Berthe Morisot, two friends of Manet who had like him become habitués of the Café Guerbois, rallied to the idea.

Thus 1874 was the year of the group's first exhibition, to which 29 artists submitted 165 paintings. Manet declined the invitation, being unable to accept its one condition: that participants should abstain from showing their work at the Official Salon. Nevertheless one thing all these young painters had in common was their admiration for Manet's work. People flocked to their exhibition, but chiefly to mock; and buyers were few and far between.
This did not prevent a repetition of the experiment. Indeed the exhibitions organized by the group, certain members of which now adopted the title of "Impressionists" which had been conferred on them by derisive critics, continued until 1886. Only Pissarro took part in every show, doggedly attempting to heal the schism which in 1879 split the group into two tendencies, led respectively by Monet and Degas.

Edouard Manet ►
Portrait of Théodore Duret (1868).
Oil on canvas:
43 x 35 cm.
Musée du Petit Palais, Paris.

Manet signed his painting upside down so that it could be admired for itself, without prejudice.

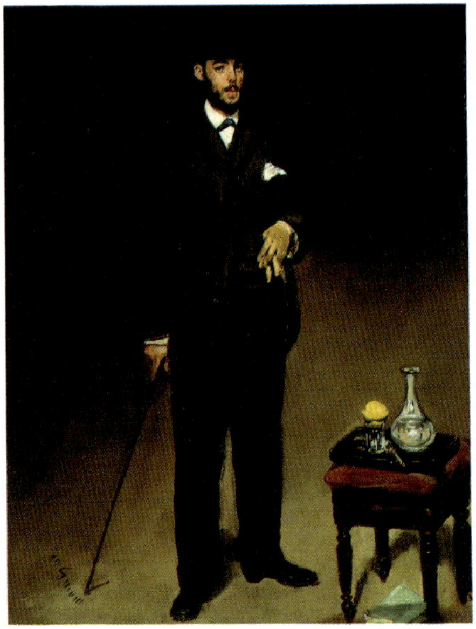

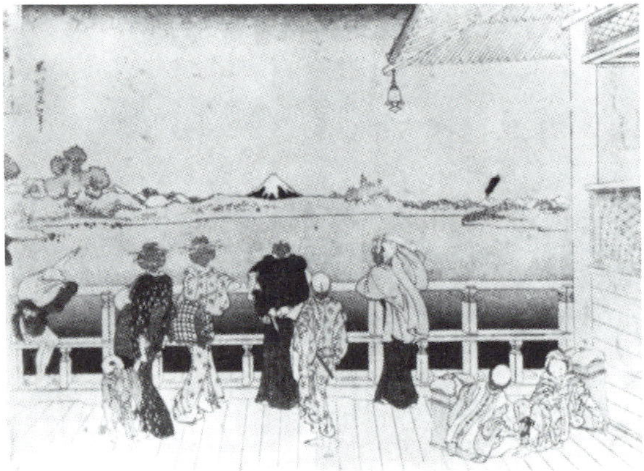

▲
Hokusai
(1760-1849).
The Sazai Pavilion, Temple of the 500 Rakans.
Print from the series
36 Views of Mount Fiji.
23.9 x 34.3 cm.
Musée Claude Monet, Giverny.

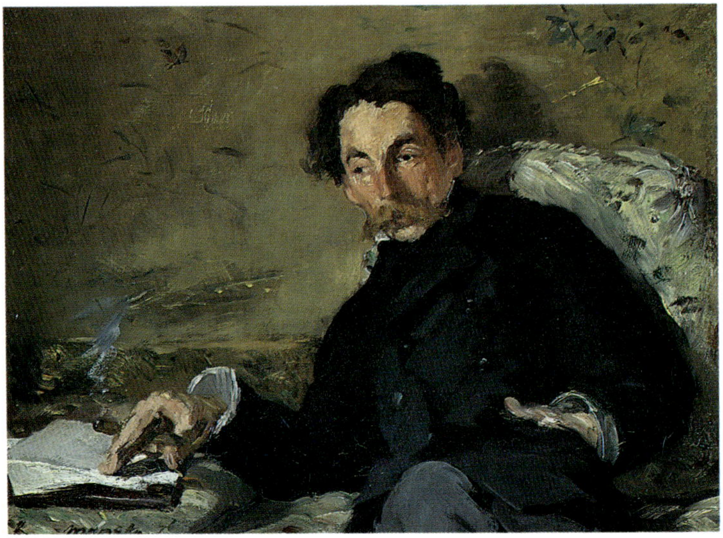

Edouard Manet ►
Portrait of Stéphane Mallarmé (1876).
Oil on canvas:
27 x 36 cm.
Musée d'Orsay, Paris.

Over the years, transcending the quarrels and deaths of its members, Impressionism came to represent the spirit of its time. Some of the Impressionists subsequently went their own ways–Degas, Renoir and Monet survived the First World War–but in general Impressionism was indelibly linked to what we know as the Belle Époque.
In effect, the movement benefitted hugely from the operations of major dealers like Durand-Ruel and Vollard. Above all it was backed by influential critics like Duret, Duranty and Mirbeau, by politicians such as Clemenceau, and by writers whom posterity now considers to have been the greatest of their time, among them Baudelaire, Zola and Mallarmé.

The high regard in which we hold the Impressionists today is largely due to these background figures, whose influence is often underestimated. They stressed the fact that the art of the Impressionists tackled a completely new set of problems and symbolized the birth of a new world to which traditional painting could no longer give expression. These were artists who rejected the established patterns, and responded to Baudelaire's challenge of creating an art that would truly reflect modern life.
To achieve this, each one of the group used the means at his own disposal. Through the diversity of styles and subjects with which they renewed the genres of portraiture, landscape painting and history painting, they showed a loyalty to certain principles which were later to give birth to modern art–namely, an opposition to convention, a desire to develop an original and personal form of art, a humble and open-minded attitude to nature, and the best possible use of the means available: canvas, brushwork, colours and surfaces.

Pierre-Auguste Renoir ▶
The Clown (1909).
Oil on canvas:
120 x 77 cm.
Musée de l'Orangerie, Paris.

Renoir seldom asked his children to sit for him, as his son Claude did here. Usually he drew inspiration from their games and their free movement, and avoided trapping them in his studio. Claude, who was eight at the time, always remembered this painting fondly, because he was kept out of school to pose for it.

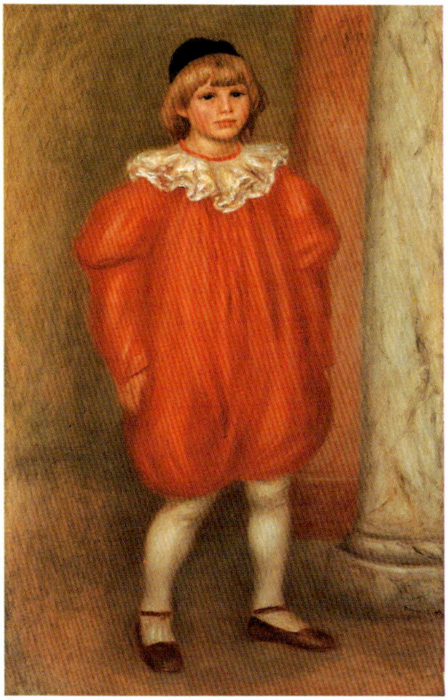

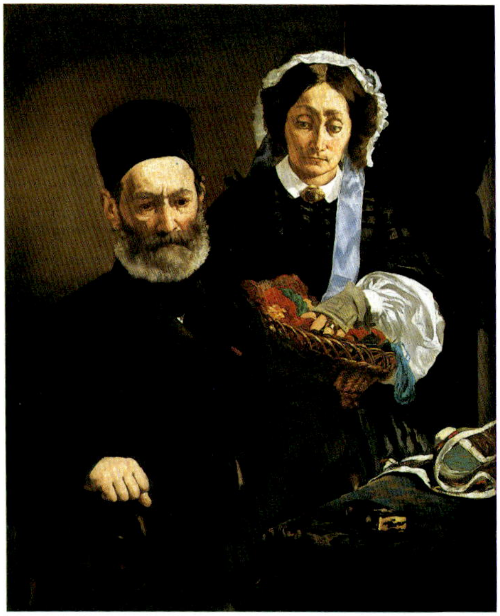

▲
Edouard Manet
Portrait of M. and Mme. Auguste Manet (1860).
Oil on canvas:
115.5 x 91 cm.
Musée d'Orsay, Paris.

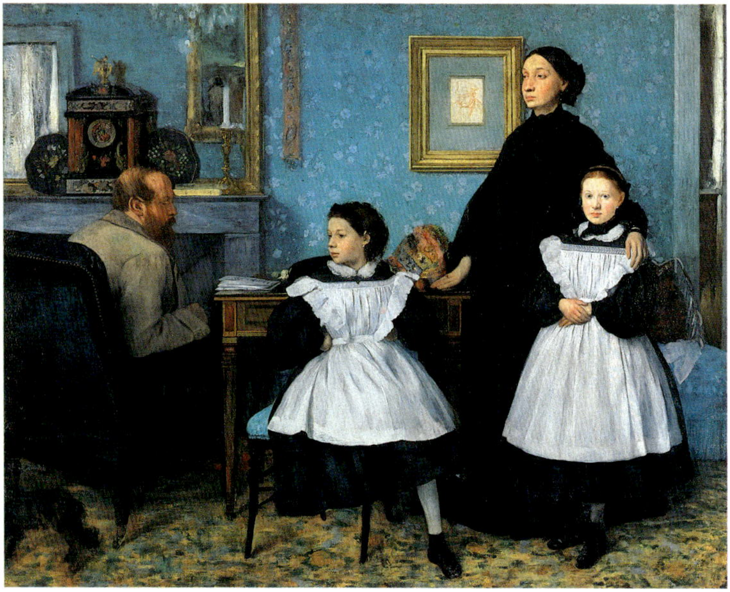

Edgar Degas ▶
(1834-1917).
Family Portait, or *The Bellelli Family*.
Begun in 1858, completed before 1867.
Oil on canvas:
200 x 250 cm.
Musée d'Orsay, Paris.

Painters of private life

The Impressionists, in their quest for a way of looking at the world that would be free of conventional encumbrances, chose the subject matter they knew best, and which they could be sure was free of outside influences. In effect they abandoned narrative and demonstrative themes and concentrated on their own private existence.
Instead of painting sumptuous, historical or dreamlike scenes, they concentrated on the places in which they actually lived, however ordinary. Instead of portraying the emperors and aristocrats of society and accepting commissions from the remote, rich and powerful, they painted their own families and even themselves. To be precise they painted the people and places they knew best.

In this way they contrived a new kind of portraiture, which no longer depended on commissions from outside and was therefore freed of the traditional constraints. To begin with, these portraits retained certain classical qualities, notably in the way the figures were posed–which was reminiscent of ceremonial portraiture–or in the way the figures were isolated against a neutral or formal background. These traits persisted for some time, but eventually gave way to an entirely new approach to the representation of the individual and his environment.

Camille Pissarro ►
(1830-1903).
Portrait of the Artist
(1873).
Oil on canvas:
56 x 46.6 cm.
Musée d'Orsay, Paris.

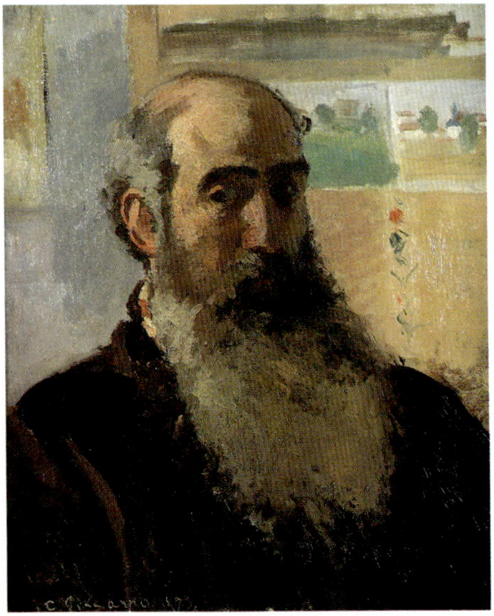

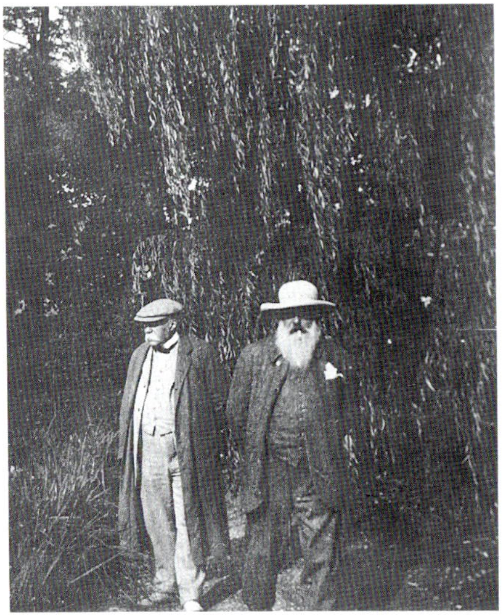

▲
Monet and Clemenceau on the Japanese Bridge at Giverny.
Photograph.

The old radical, sanctified by his role as France's victorious wartime leader, is here shown visiting Monet, his friend of 30 years. In 1879, another friend, Manet, had painted Clemenceau's portrait.

Paul Cézanne ►
(1839-1906).
Portrait of Ambroise Vollard (1899).
Oil on canvas:
100 x 81 cm.
Musée du Petit Palais, Paris.

In 1895, Ambroise Vollard organized Cézanne's first one-man exhibition. Cézanne's portrait of Vollard took up 115 sittings before it was finally abandoned– in its present form.

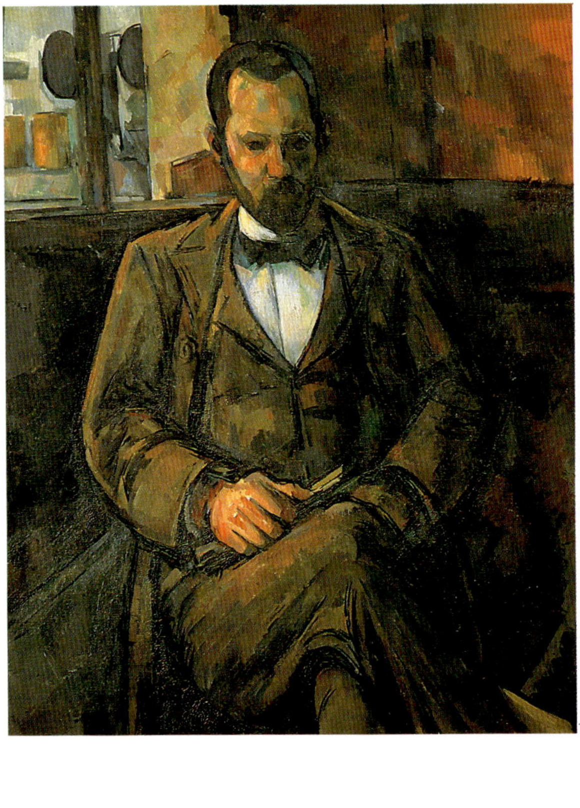

This concept arose from a wish to show private people and places as they were, without using them as a vehicle for some general idea or moral precept. The Impressionist painter tended to work in his own home, or in the homes of his friends and relations. He painted what he saw, warts and all, without adornment.
The scope of this scrupulous process of observation covered the whole of private life. The artist portrayed not only his own family, but also his professional colleagues and the people he frequented from day to day.
From this intimate, banal approach, he fashioned a painting which was its own raison d'être, without pretending to be a psychological study.
Since he was no longer concerned with capturing the characters of his models, he ran the risk of confining himself to the exterior aspects of people and situations. But by restricting himself to the plane of intimacy, he mitigated this danger by an inner knowledge of his subject, which was plainly perceptible in the painting.

In this way his whole attention was focussed on reproducing on canvas exactly what his eye revealed. The truth of man was no longer to be found in his soul (which the artist had previously to suggest); it lay in the way nature affected his features, and in the way his physical and social environment moulded him.
At the same time, when the same subject was tirelessly represented over and over, it ended by vanishing altogether, becoming no more than an excuse for pictural effects. These, paradoxically, revealed the essence of the subject better than more traditional means of representation.

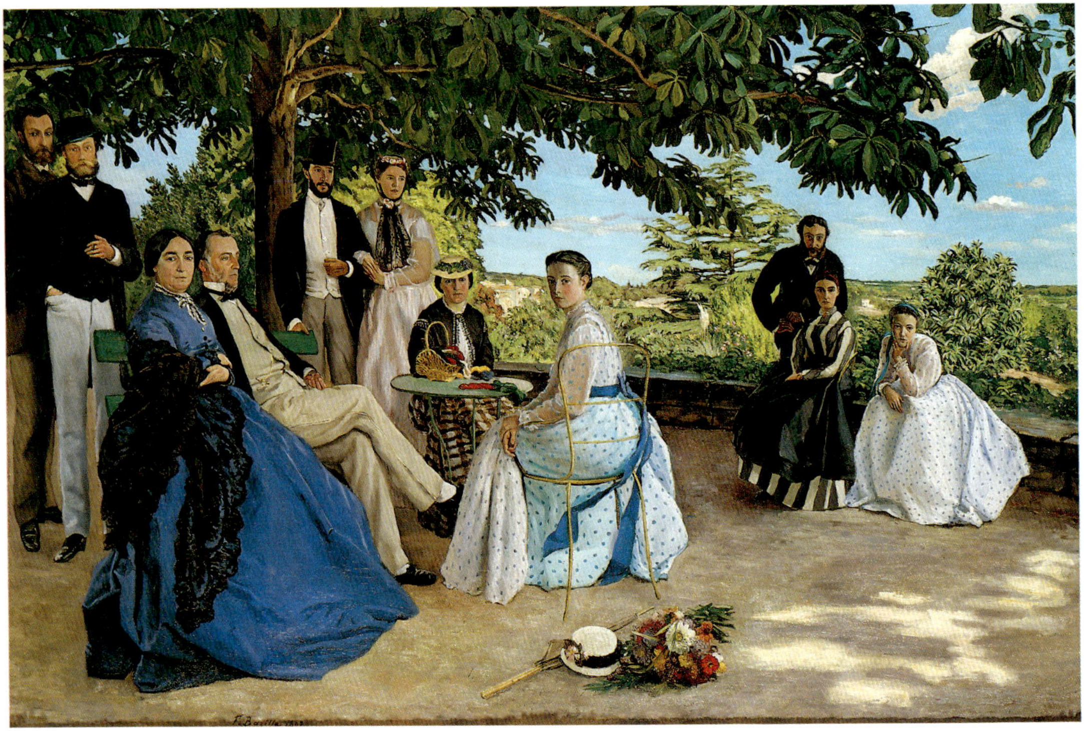

▲
Frédéric Bazille
(1841-1870).
Family Reunion
(1867).
Oil on canvas:
152 x 230 cm.
Musée d'Orsay, Paris.

FREDERIC BAZILLE

family portraits

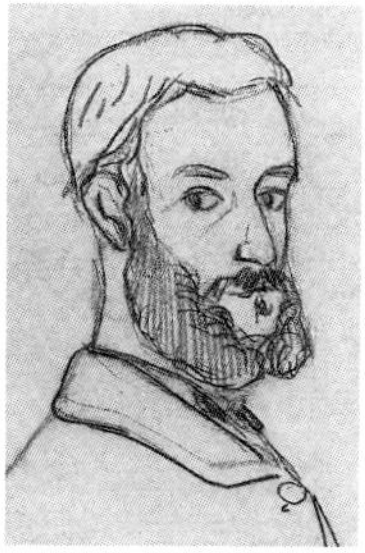

▲
Frédéric Bazille
Self-Portait, detail.
Black stone:
24.1 x 34.5 cm.
Musée du Louvre,
Paris.

Eleven figures are shown in small separate groups, in a long horizontal format. Although the title of the painting indicates that this is a 'reunion', the participants do not appear to communicate with one another in any way. Rather than a group portrait, this is a group of portraits.

Each individual wears a simple costume, the typical uniform of the wealthy country bourgeoisie at the end of the Second Empire. It is summer, and the relatives of the artist (Bazille has painted himself at the far left) are shown on the terrace of one of their properties near Montpellier. The place and the people shown are intimately connected to one another–yet the atmosphere is cold.

remoteness and intimacy

The picture has been painstakingly executed, with the gravity which was Bazille's trademark. The colour is laid on in broad zones which give the series of faces a frieze-like appearance. The artist has not tried to achieve any psychological insight; he remains aloof in his description of the scene.
The pools of light on the right, the leaves of the tree that overspreads the tableau, the translucent blue of the sky and the still life in the foreground, seem to be as important as the figures themselves. The portraits do not have any pre-established function. For his painting, Bazille only uses people of whom he is fond, and who are consequently highly available as subjects.

A young man of good family
Bazille, who collaborated frequently with Renoir and Monet, went back to stay with his family every summer, painting numerous portraits of them in the landscapes he knew best.

the family as subject matter

With the exception of Renoir, the Impressionists almost never painted portraits on commission, preferring to use the people closest to them as models. Because their chief goal was to represent exactly what they saw, they did not try to define the characters of their subjects, much less some mysterious soul within them, whose existence they anyway did not acknowledge.

models free of charge

In the early 1860's, the future Impressionists were still painting the professional models who came to pose in the academies they attended. Later, their chronic lack of funds obliged them to stick to the free (and usually available) models furnished by their immediate families. They painted them just as they were, doing everyday things in everyday clothes.

A picnic with friends
Two years after the furore provoked by Manet's *Luncheon on the Grass*, Monet paid homage to his master by painting his own version of the same theme in the Fontainebleau woods. Among the figures are Bazille (in a bowler hat) and Monet's mistress Camille Doncieux. This huge canvas was later cut into several pieces.

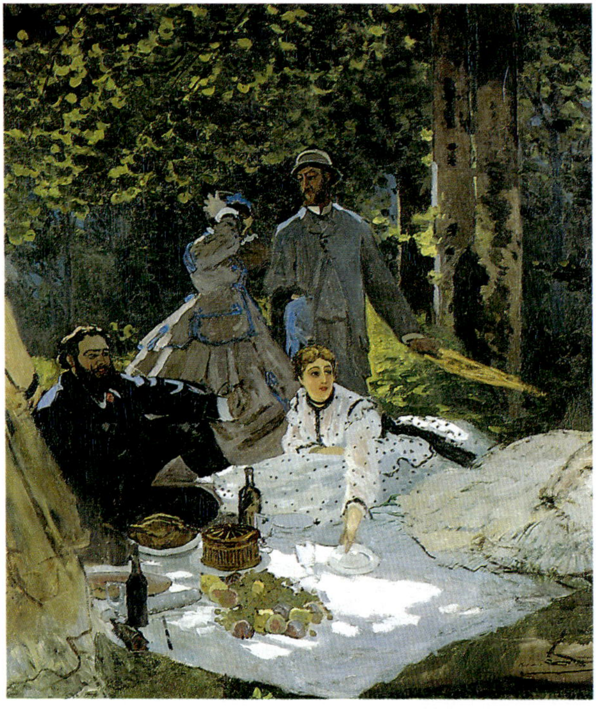

◄ **Claude Monet**
Luncheon on the Grass
(1865-1866).
Oil on canvas:
248 x 217 cm.
Musée d'Orsay, Paris.

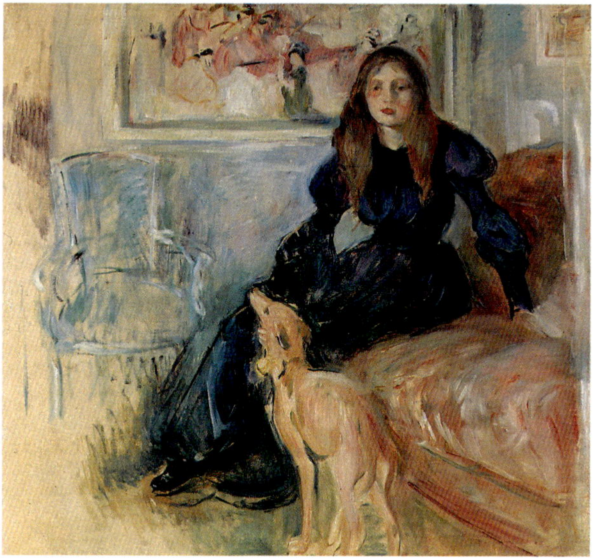

Berthe Morisot (1841-1895). *Julie Manet and her greyhound Laertes* (1893). Oil on canvas: 73 x 80 cm. Musée Marmottan, Paris.

Julie, Morisot's daughter, gave this picture to Monet as a souvenir after her mother's death.

The habit of a lifetime
When Monet saw his wife Camille on her deathbed in 1879, he was deeply moved– but still couldn't refrain from noting the blues, yellows and greys imprinted by death on the face of this woman, whom he had painted in the flower of her youth as the central figure in *Luncheon on the Grass*.

After they became successful and their work became prized by collectors, they carried on painting their families, whom they could observe on a daily basis. The artist's consort, with her children, was always a favourite subject for the portraits of Monet, Renoir and Cézanne. There could be no substitute for long association with a person, if one wanted to express the way it was changed by its environment.
The subject is invariably integrated with a décor, into which he or she has a tendency to melt. The way in which the artist chooses to point up some details, while others are handled in a more cursory manner, has little to do with their symbolic importance; instead it demonstrates how the eye's focus of intensity varies with distance. Even against an apparently neutral background, as in the later portraits of Cézanne, the shapes and colours making up the figures are scrupulously blended with the surroundings.

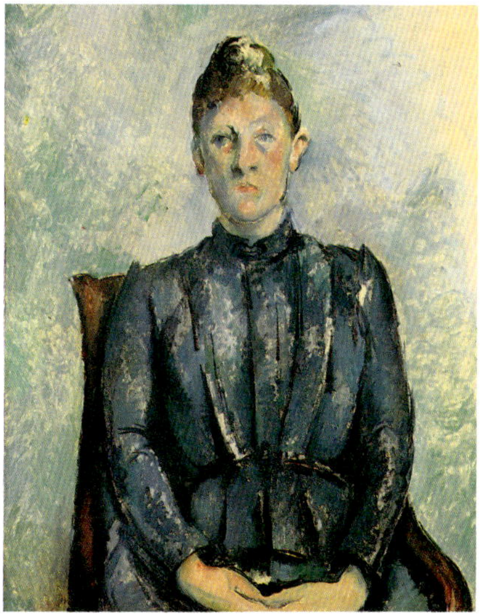

Paul Cézanne *Portrait of Madame Cézanne* (1885-1890). Oil on canvas: 81 x 65 cm. Musée de l'Orangerie, Paris.

friends and models

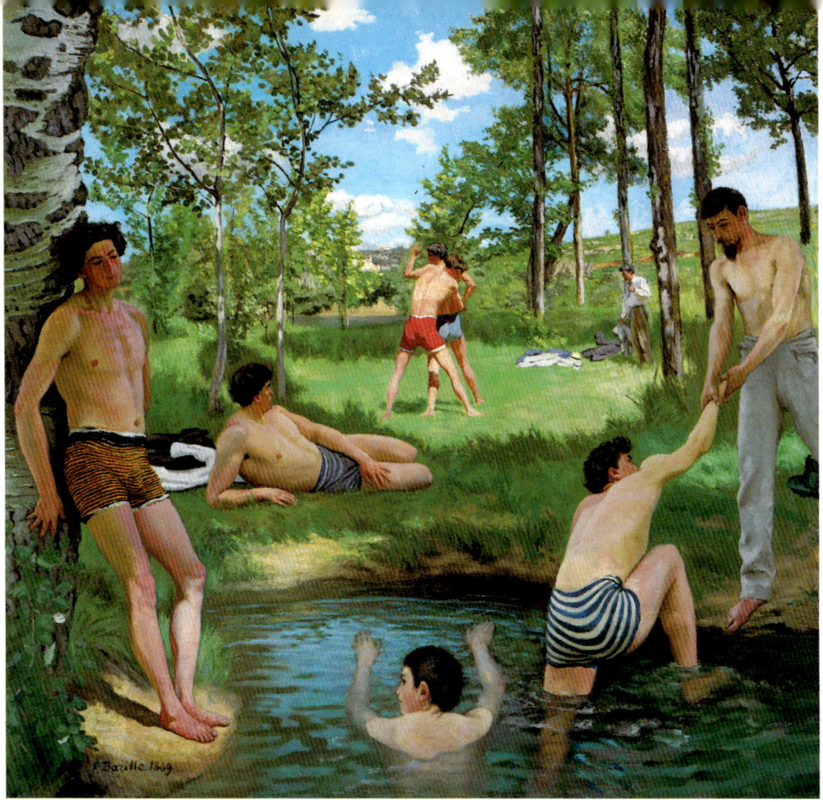

▲ **Frédéric Bazille**
Scene in summer (1869).
Oil on canvas: 158 x 159 cm.
Fogg Art Museum, Cambridge, USA.

This canvas, painted shortly before his death, was the first public success achieved by Bazille. It blends observations made in the open air of bathers near Montpellier, with studies, from life, of poses reminiscent of the classical themes of St Sebastian, and of Jacob wrestling with the angel.

Grandeur and banality
Paradoxically, for some of the Impressionists the goal was to confer grandeur on the ordinary by giving it artistic status. To achieve this, Manet, Bazille and Cézanne painted many figures in their scenes of everyday life in poses borrowed from traditional mythology.

The circle of intimates painted by the artist usually extended well beyond his own family–except in the case of Cézanne, who lived most of his life in isolation at Aix (he would occasionally come back to Paris to horrify the regulars at the Café Guerbois with his exaggerated boorishness)–and Berthe Morisot, who could scarcely go out of her house if she wished to retain her status as an "honest woman". With these two exceptions, the Impressionists were a highly sociable crowd, as their pictures testify.
Manet and Degas, both of whom were bachelors, did many portraits of their acquaintances, many of whom were important figures in the intellectual and social worlds of Paris in the late 19th century. Manet painted several portraits of writers who were his friends, like Mallarmé, Baudelaire and Zola. Degas produced many likenesses of Ludovic Halévy, who wrote librettos for the operettas of Offenbach, and worked with him to

direct *La Cigale*, a ferocious satire on the Impressionist painters. Thus he was able to make a prime subject of a man who had a part in both his professional and his private life.

a fresh approach to convention

Sometimes these pictures reflect the conventional portrait of the writer surrounded by his attributes, the way it has been ever since the Renaissance. But these conventions are used in a different way, as in the case of Bazille or Manet, who raised the banal to the level of the huge historical compositions in the Louvre. This tactic did not work very well in the last analysis, and post-1870 "historical" portraits of the Impressionists became indistinguishable from their family ones.

Edgar Degas
Portraits of friends on stage (Ludovic Halévy and Albert Cavé) (1879).
Pastel and distemper on paper:
79 x 55 cm.
Musée d'Orsay, Paris.
▼

Edouard Manet
Portrait of Emile Zola (1868).
Oil on canvas:
146 x 114 cm.
Musée d'Orsay, Paris.
▼

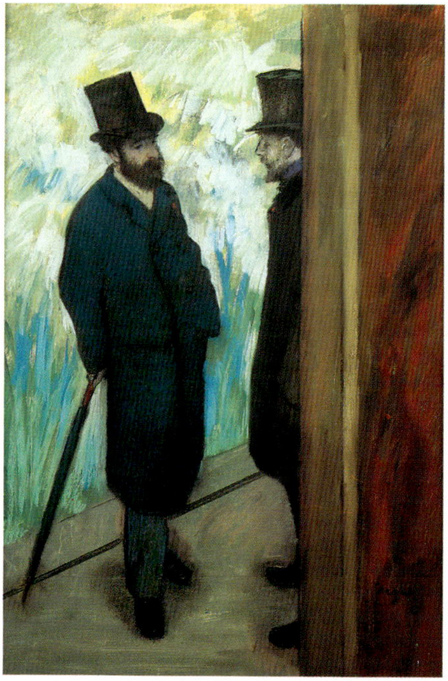

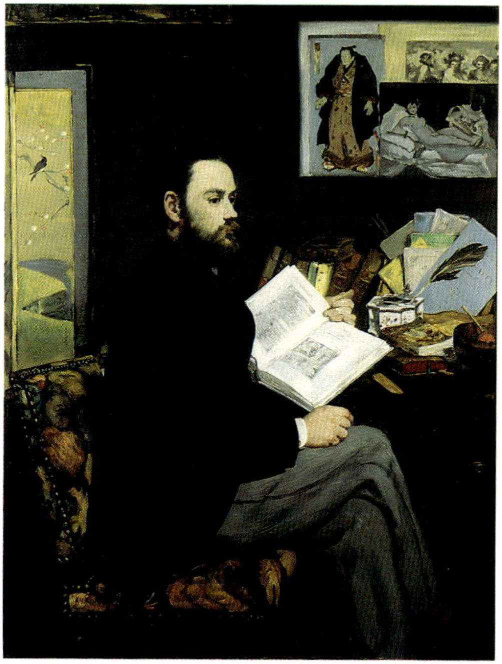

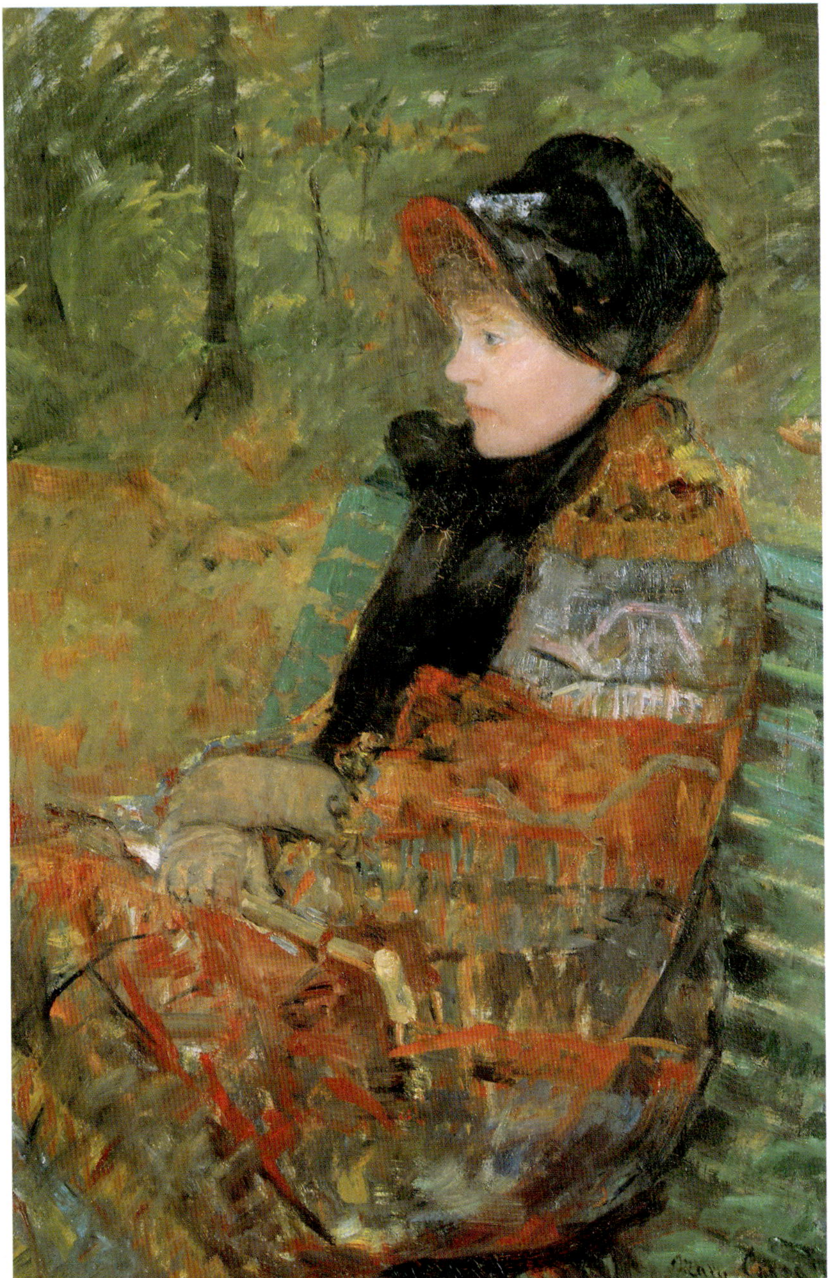

MARY CASSATT

ordinary men and women

A young girl sits on a bench under the trees. In no way does she look like a woman of the world who has commissioned a painter to do her portrait; nor is she naked, or otherwise psychologically scrutinized by the artist. This image is no longer the traditional image of women, it is the picture of an ordinary woman.

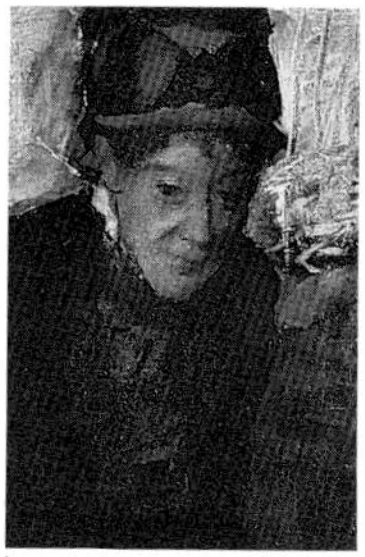

▲ **Edgar Degas**
Miss Cassatt seated, with cards
(about 1884), detail.
Oil on canvas:
71.5 x 58.7 cm.
National Portrait Gallery, Washington.

The face of Lydia Cassatt, the artist's sister, is the only thoroughly crafted element in the picture (with the exception of the gloved hands). The delicacy of the colouring suggests volume, while the eye and mouth are rendered to achieve an exact likeness. The remainder of the composition is handled in thick, woolly textures, with tones heightened by occasional pink and bright blue touches. The cane resting on the model's knees is no more than a slightly longer brushstroke than those around it.

An American in Paris
The American painter Mary Cassatt came to Paris with her family, which supplied her with her principal models after her friend Degas convinced her to abandon academicism. She painted many portraits of her sister Lydia, who died in 1882.

an equal focus on both model and painting

The painting is based on an uncertain balance between two poles. The eye is simultaneously drawn by the handling of the brushwork and by the precision of the face. It cannot linger on the character of the model, but neither can that character be entirely ignored. The girl is only of real importance to the picture in so far as the artist has contrived to extract from her an unusual wealth of interest, without in any way detracting from her simplicity.

◄ **Mary Cassatt**
(1844-1926).
Autumn, or Portrait of Miss. C. (Lydia Cassat)
(1880).
Oil on canvas:
92.5 x 65.4 cm.
Musée du Petit Palais, Paris.

Mary Cassatt's women

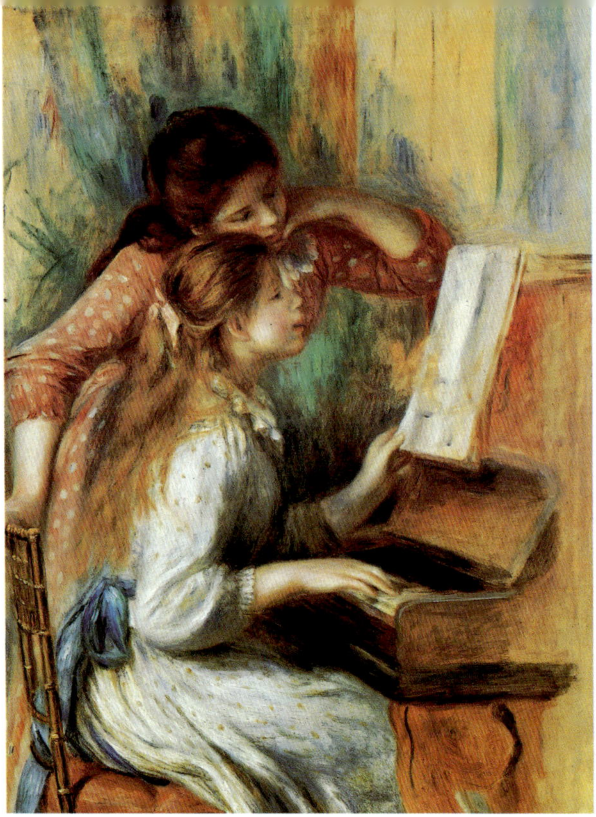

◄ **Pierre-Auguste Renoir**
Girls playing the piano (1892).
Oil on canvas: 116 x 81 cm.
Musée de l'Orangerie, Paris.

Renoir painted six versions of this picture. The fresh handling and the elegance of the poses express all the charm of bourgeois family life.

"Miss Cassatt has shown us a woman functioning in real terms, as the mistress of her home, and as a mother... she has enriched these topics with her art."
A. Mellerio, 1893.

Women and children were always the principal subjects of Mary Cassatt. The same was true of Berthe Morisot, the only woman who took part in the first Impressionist Exhibition of 1877. That she was the only one was no doubt due to the entrenched tradition that women painters were tolerated on condition that they stuck to still lives or family portraiture. For Morisot and Cassatt the goal was to paint original subjects and to transmit their own experience of life, rather than conform to the restrictions imposed by a male-dominated society.

an everyday enchantment

Mary Cassatt, though she was herself unmarried, made motherhood one of her central themes. She seldom painted *femmes du monde* of her own kind, preferring the models she found within her own family or in the families of her village. For Berthe Morisot, who was

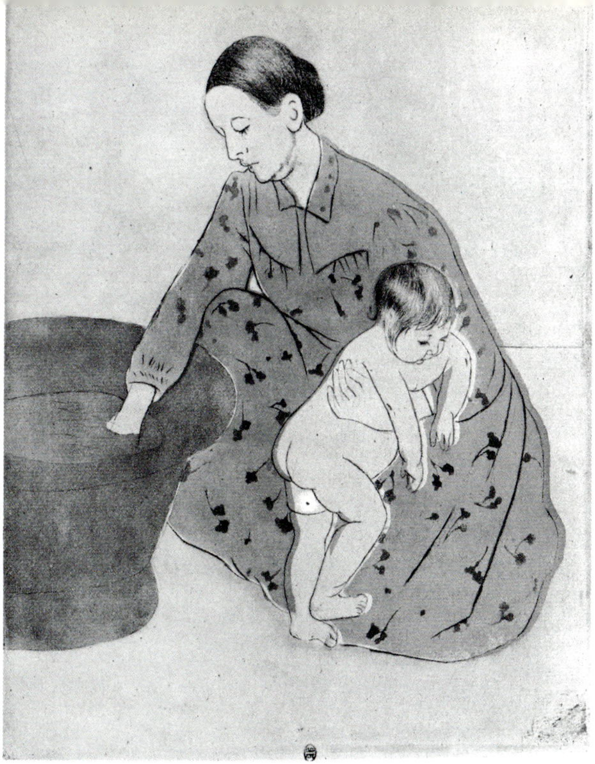

◄ **Mary Cassatt**
The Bath (1890-91).
Etchers' point:
31.9 x 24.9 cm.
Bibliothèque
Nationale, Paris.

married to Eugène Manet, the brother of the painter who had been her teacher, women in their domestic surroundings were natural subjects. She did not confine herself to women, but as Mallarmé noted she was able to conjure up their "everyday enchantment".

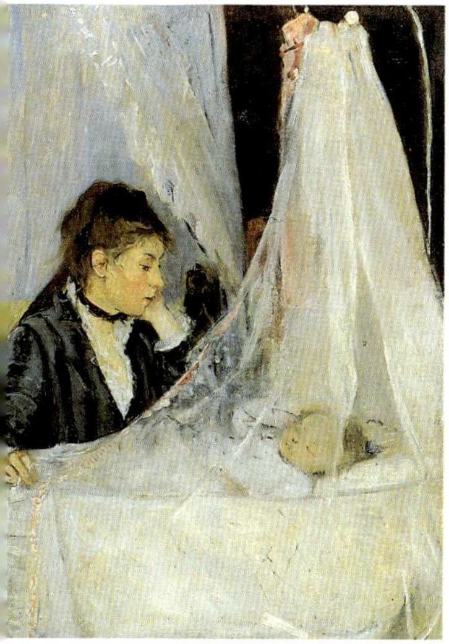

◄ **Berthe Morisot**
The cradle (1872).
Oil on canvas:
56 x 46 cm.
Musée d'Orsay, Paris.

The painter's sister, exquisitely portrayed, bends tenderly over the cradle of her newborn daughter, whose features are barely defined.

no more moralizing

Women and children of the period were no longer used as pretexts for moral strictures–nor even for illustrating bourgeois family virtues in the manner of Renoir, given that the children in Impressionist paintings tend more often to be accompanied by their nurses than by their mothers. By far the strongest emphasis was on quiet intimacy and tender, even sugary sentiment; whatever we may think, art gained a lot from this calming influence.

the spectator in the frame

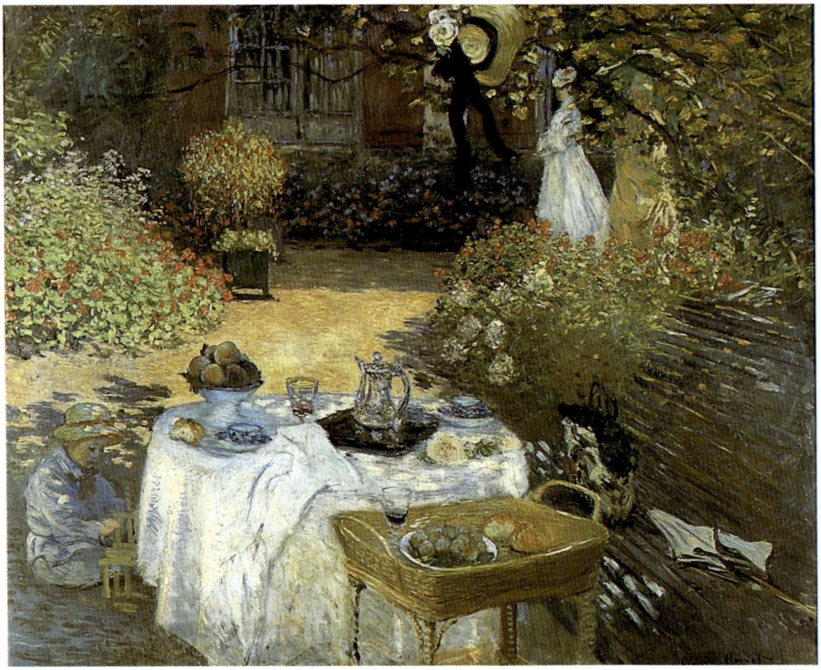

▲
Claude Monet
The Luncheon (1873).
Oil on canvas:
162 x 203 cm.
Musée d'Orsay, Paris.

In Monet's garden at Argenteuil, his son Jean is shown playing beside the table which the two women in the background have just left.

The Impressionists' interest in painting members of their families, especially those who were traditionally neglected (women and children), did not spring from introspection. In the eyes of these artists, proximity to the things of this world was best described by their daily lives at home. What they meant to communicate–and celebrate–was their love of nature's more prosaic aspect.

the sharing of intimacy

To do this, they were not content to paint detached scenes of their home interiors, incorporating people, décors and objects that happened to be within their range as they worked. The intimate character of what they painted was emphasized by the intimate character of its presentation. Frequently these pictures are composed in such a way that the observer finds himself enveloped by the scene.

Gustave Caillebotte ►
(1848-1894)
The Luncheon (1876).
Oil on canvas:
52 x 75 cm.
Private Collection.

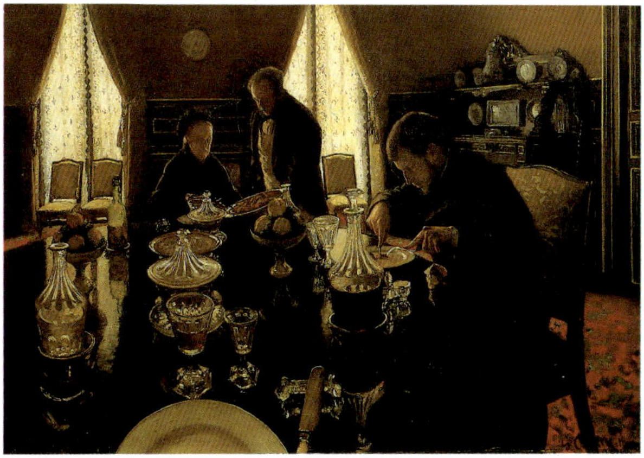

Edgar Degas
Woman drying her neck after bathing
(about 1895).
Pastel on cardboard:
62.2 x 65 cm.
Musée d'Orsay, Paris.

Degas portrayed women at their toilet hundreds of times over. It was his way of exposing to us all that which all of us conceal.
▼

The family meal taken in the privacy of the home was a favourite–and universal–theme that projected domestic intimacy. The Impressionists took the fullest advantage of the possibilities it offered, both in atmosphere and in perspective. In many of the paintings they produced on this theme, a table is placed in the foreground, cut off by the frame, as if part of it projected into the room containing the painting, and as if the onlooker were himself seated at it. Degas used the same approach in his bath scenes, which under normal circumstances were completely private. The Impressionists used similar shortcuts of perspective to highlight the intimate quality in other subjects, some of them bordering on the voyeuristic. The paintings they produced seem to assimilate themselves into our space, whilst we ourselves penetrate almost physically into theirs; thus both dimensions merge into the single world of everyday human life.

"These pastels show the stumps of cripples, the throats of scolds and the swaying of legless torsos–a whole series of attitudes inherent to woman when she is young, pretty, adorable, whether recumbent or upright... in this case, the woman bends to conceal the beauty she has lost, in the act of combing her hair."
J-K. Huysmans,
1889.

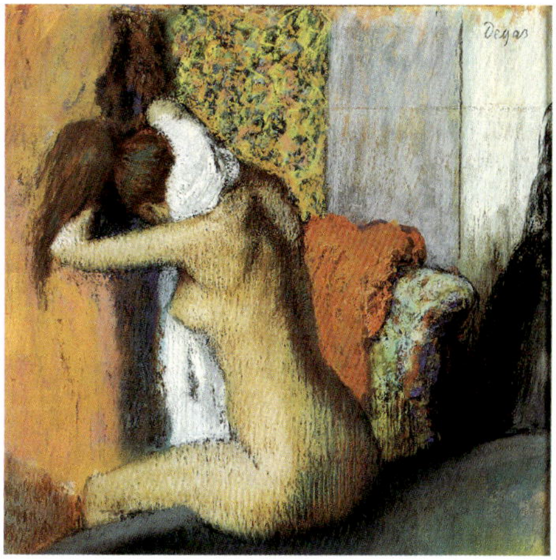

Edouard Manet
The Escape of Rochefort
(1880-1881).
Oil on canvas:
80 x 73 cm.
Musée d'Orsay, Paris.

Manet undertook this picture in celebration of the amnesty granted to the left-wing hero Henri Rochefort, a journalist banished by Napoleon III. All we see of Rochefort's escape is the sea, and one dark dot on a horizon crowded with indistinct outlines. ►

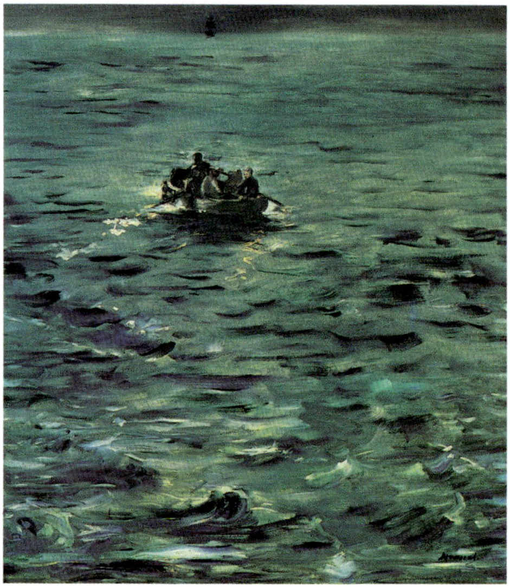

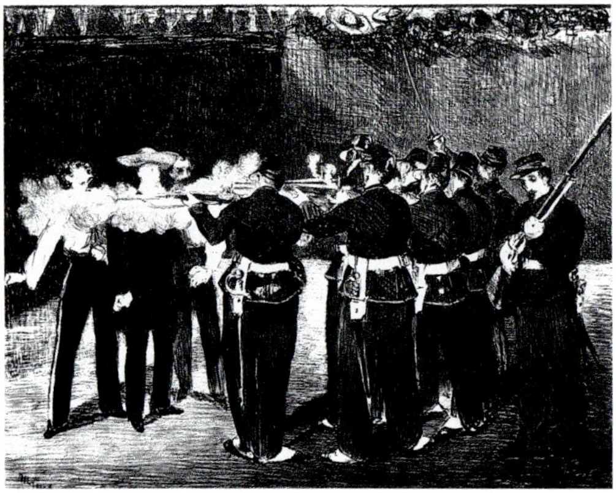

◄ **Edouard Manet**
The Execution of Maximilian
(1868).
Lithograph:
33.3 x 43.3 cm.
Bibliothèque Nationale,
Paris.

One of several pictures on this subject painted by Manet, in which a historic event is so tightly crammed into the space available to it that it loses its pathos.

Edgar Degas ►
Spartan girls taunting boys
(begun about 1860, completed before 1880).
Oil on canvas:
109 x155 cm.
National Gallery,
London.

The only ancient Greek details in this picture are the costumes of the figures in the background.

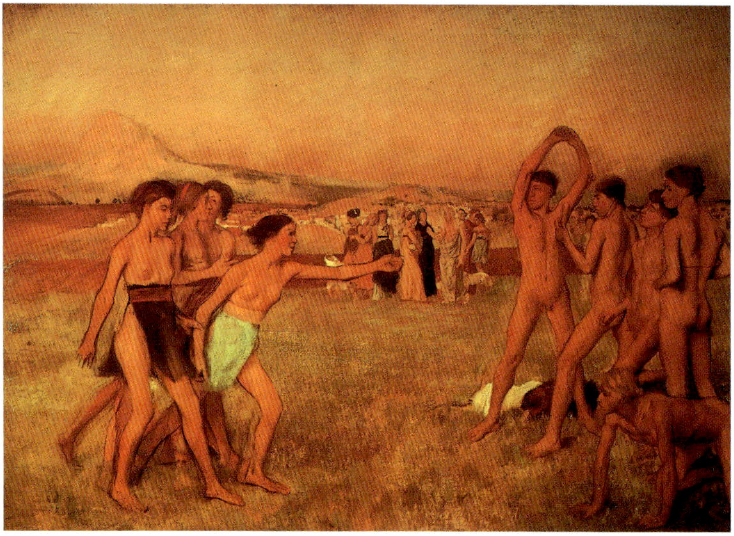

Painters of modern life

In the 19th-century hierarchy of subjects for art, mythology and history were pre-eminent, the *sine qua non* of success at the Salon. Some of the Impressionists had attempted these themes in their early careers, to impress the critics and achieve success. Others, like Monet, steadfastly refused to do so.

Manet saw himself as a pupil of Thomas Couture, a painter celebrated for his monumental work *Romans in the era of Decadence* (1846). Degas venerated Ingres and vaunted his master's love of antiquity. More out of loyalty to their own time than out of clumsiness, both men flatly declined to produce thoroughgoing history paintings. Manet persisted to the end with an ambition to depict the epoch-making events of his lifetime, such as the Mexican Revolution, the riots in Paris and the tumult surrounding the foundation of the Third Republic.

But because he rejected narrative convention he was never able to do so. Henceforth, as Baudelaire understood so well, there was no more need to go foraging in the past for subject matter, or even to seek out new themes. Reality could now be taken at face value and endowed with its true grandeur, hitherto concealed.

Edgar Degas
At the Café, also called *Absinthe* (1875-1876).
Oil on canvas:
92 x 68 cm.
Musée d'Orsay, Paris.

Ellen Andrée, a friend of Degas and the model for this picture, commented later: "I'm sitting with a glass of absinthe, and Desboutins opposite has some perfectly innocent brew. Preposterous!" The effect is heightened by the audacity of Degas' perspective and brushwork, along with the succession of tables which seem to float in space. ►

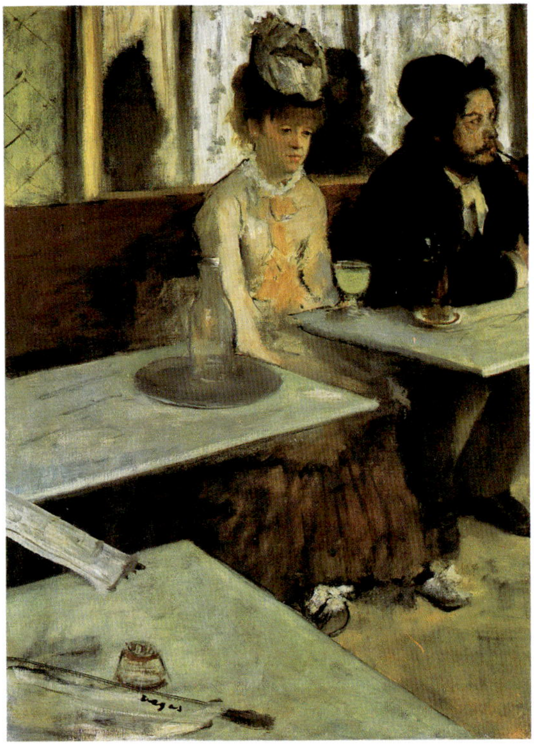

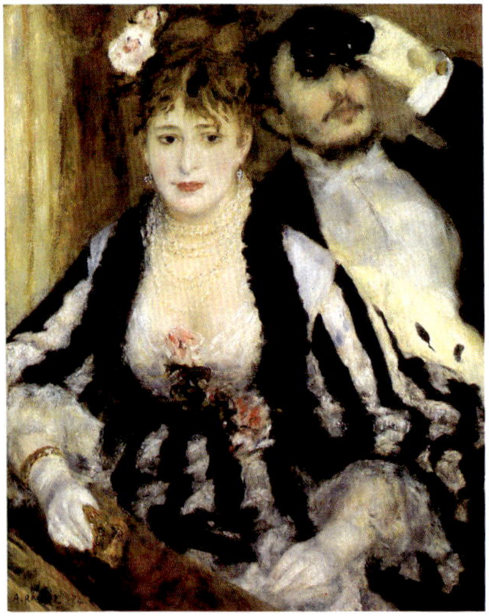

▲
Pierre-Auguste Renoir
The Box (1874).
Oil on canvas:
80 x 63 cm.
Courtauld Institute Galleries, London.

"... one of those rare paintings in which everything is enchanting, surprising, new and unexpected, inviting comparison with the greatest masterpieces."
A. André, 1931.

►
Edgar Degas
Amateur jockeys at the races
(begun 1876, completed 1887).
Oil on canvas:
66 x 81cm.
Musée d'Orsay, Paris.

Fields, steam locomotive, jockeys in their bright colours, figures sporting the latest style in hats... the races clearly offer a meeting of very different worlds.

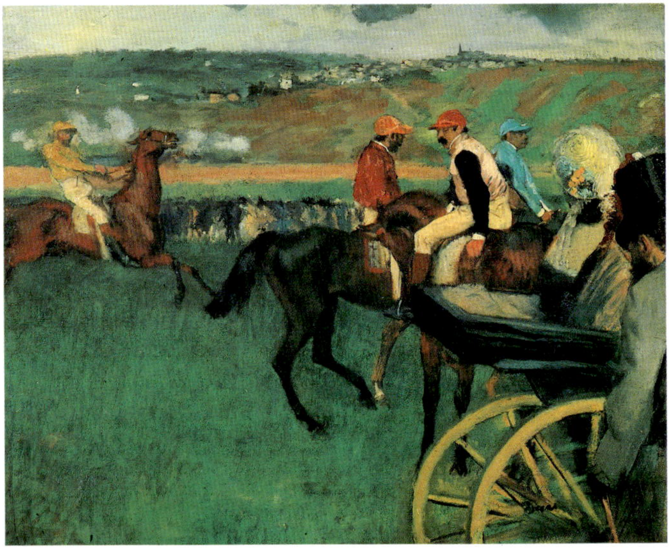

In 1863, Baudelaire wrote of "the painter of modern life" who would "... try to squeeze from fashion whatever it might contain of poetry, in the historic sense", and who would "extract the eternal from the transitory". The Impressionists responded loyally to this injunction. In his way, each one of them used his preferred subject-matter to capture the "modernity" of the time. The urgency of the task was very great, given that society was already grappling with radical changes and profound political upheavals. With the foundering of the Republic in 1871, it was the newer, less rigid society of the middle class which came to the fore.

The world depicted by the Impressionists was no longer immutable. Their refusal to dress their figures in antique costumes, their rejection of exotic, eternal decors and their insistence on details which pinpointed their pictures in temporal and social reality–all stemmed from the fact that both man and his environment had changed completely.
Modern life is instability and perpetual transformation. The Impressionists set out to paint cafés, theatres and cabarets where the scandalous *demi-monde* met and mingled. Nor did they shrink from showing the reverse of the medal, a world of work which encompassed every character-type from the labourer to the rich financier.
In this way they set out (with varying degrees of constancy and conscientiousness) to explore the emergent new society; the old references had become unworkable, and there was a clear need for new ones.

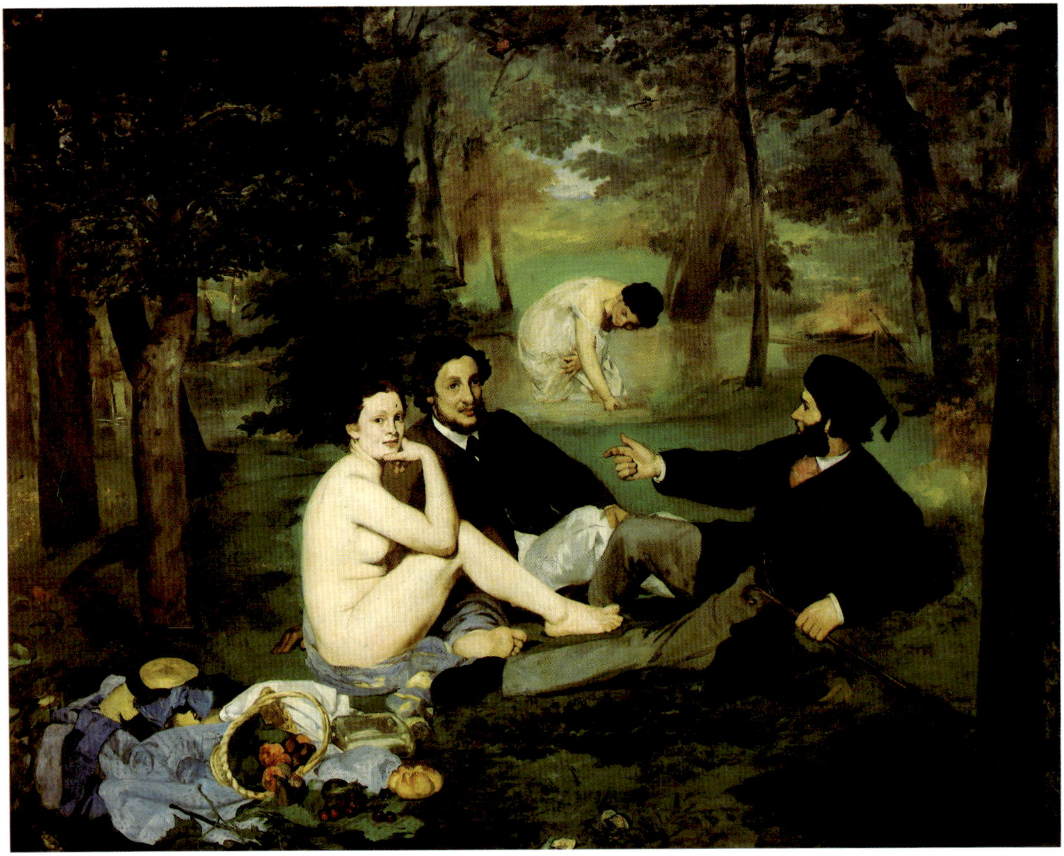

▲
Edouard Manet
(1832- 1883).
Luncheon on the Grass
(1863).
Oil on canvas:
208 x 264 cm.
Musée d'Orsay.

EDOUARD MANET

the invention of modern painting

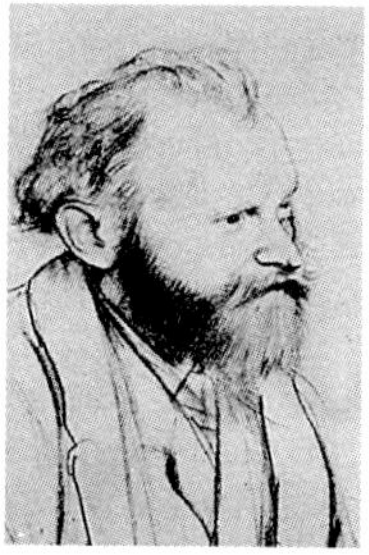

▲
Edgar Degas
Manet seated
(around 1864), detail.
Drawing.
Metropolitan
Museum, New York.

In this painting a nude woman is shown sitting with two men in city clothes. *Luncheon on the Grass* caused a furore at the Salon des Refusés in 1863, and Napoleon III himself called it an "insult to modesty". Today, Manet's picture has lost none of its power to shock, even though our reactions to it are no longer quite so prudish.

The different groups of objects and figures in the painting seem unconnected. Manet stated that he had set out to paint a "modern Giorgione"; and indeed the poses of the models are copied from various Renaissance masterworks. But still *Luncheon on the Grass* is really a collection of references, without real affinities.

"Manet realised the dream of all painters: that of placing lifesize figures in a landscape... This nude scandalised the public... which thought it unlike anything ever seen before. And this was a great error, because at the Louvre there are over fifty paintings in which clothed figures are mixed with naked ones. But nobody goes sniffing after scandal in the Louvre."
É. Zola, 1867.

a collage of fragments

This fragmentary quality is increased by the disparity of the handling. The still life in the foreground is done with an eye to relief and precise details, while the figures themselves appear flat against the surface. Manet is clearly playing a game, using all the resources at his disposal; the picture is really a 'foursome', played out between the protagonists in the scene and between the elements which make possible the composition of a work of art. "*The Foursome*" (*La partie carrée*) was indeed his private title for the picture.
Classical art–i.e. antiquity rendered prosaic, in which the nude has inadvertently mislaid her clothes–is here brutally conjoined with contemporary art; the suited figure is in itself a sufficient subject for a picture, no less worthy of our attention than a god of mythology.

Manet's legacy of painting

The brand of modernity which in 1863 aroused such an outcry against this and nearly every other painting by Manet, is exactly what has given his work its unique place in art history. The "defects" of Manet were to become the standards of modern art. His painting is unfinished, it tells no story, it does not attempt to put a gloss on reality. Above all, it glories in the fact that it has no unity.

a landmark...

Here, as in *Olympia*, Manet suggests a new attitude to sexuality, to the relationship between the artist and his model, and to the way in which society is built on complex male-female relationships. For example the naked woman in the trio is clearly a professional who has just removed her clothes and will certainly put them on again when the sitting is over. Manet is also

Felix Vallotton ▶
(1865-1925)
Black girl and white girl
(1913).
Oil on canvas:
114 x 147 cm.
Private collection.

Forty years after the fact, Vallotton rendered this sardonic homage to Manet's Olympia.

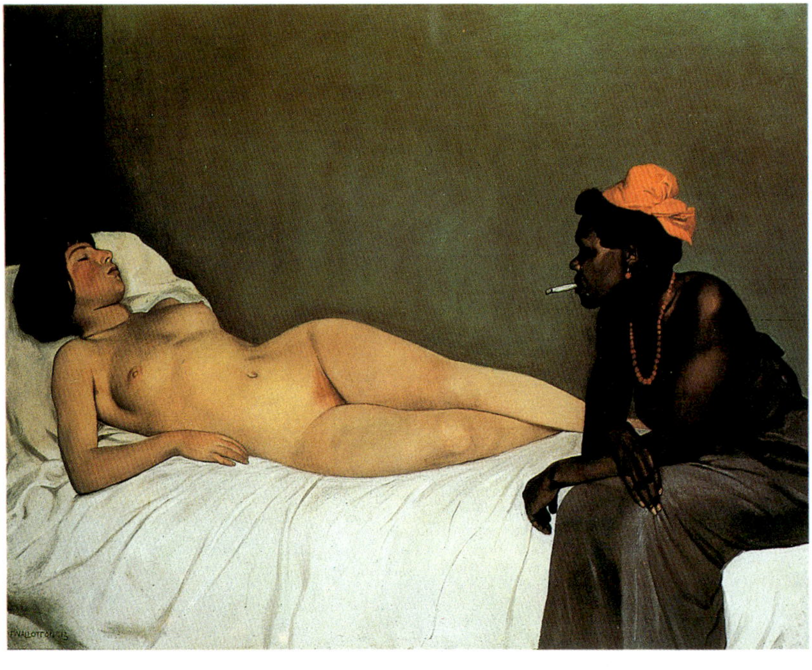

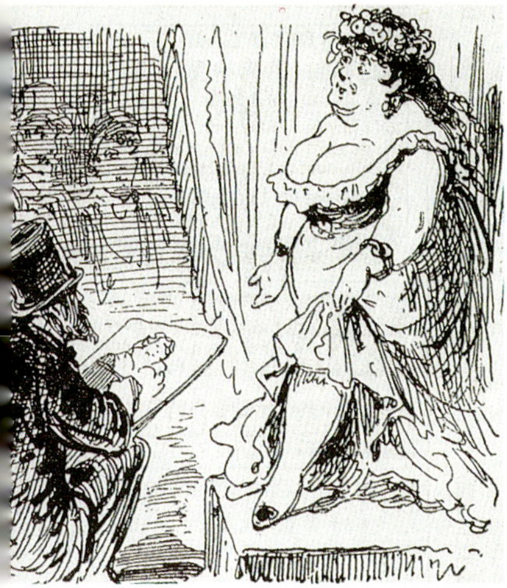

very forthright about his methods. *Luncheon on the Grass* is a kind of patchwork, an assemblage of densely-coloured brushstrokes which actually draw the eye and the attention away from the objects they are supposed to represent. The fabric of the picture has become a subject in itself, just like the fabric of society.

◄ *"M. Manet studying the beauties of nature".* Caricature in the satirical review *Le Charivari,* April 25, 1880.

...for modern art

Manet, having borrowed his methods and his subject matter from others, was himself copied by an extraordinary number of later artists, each of whom interpreted the master's modernity in his own way. Manet presents us with a picnic as a fact of society. Cézanne injected the theme with eroticism, along with a certain violence. And for a succession of abstract artists like Frank Stella and Claude Viallat, *Luncheon on the Grass* represented a call to abandon all objectives in favour of the material aspects of creation. Finally, Picasso produced several dozen overtly sexual variations on Manet's picture between 1959 and 1962.

"In the abode of beauty, in the rarefied world of art, the sudden appearance of "what we really seem" was an overwhelming event and from it was born the secret play of light and technique which is modern art. This art could render anybody, and everything, majestic... provided they belonged to that which is, as revealed by the power of paint."
G. Bataille, 1955.

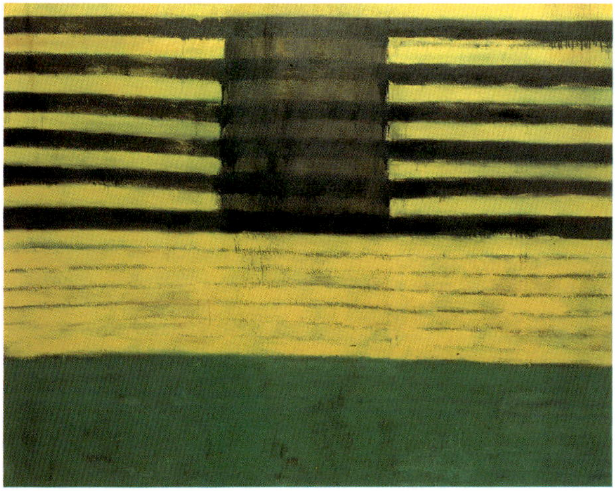

◄ **Frank Stella** (1936)
Seward Park (1958). Oil on canvas: 215.5 x 278 x 7.7 cm. Kunstmuseum, Basel.

As a young American painter, Stella used Manet's colours and composition, but eliminated the figures.

Manet and human realities

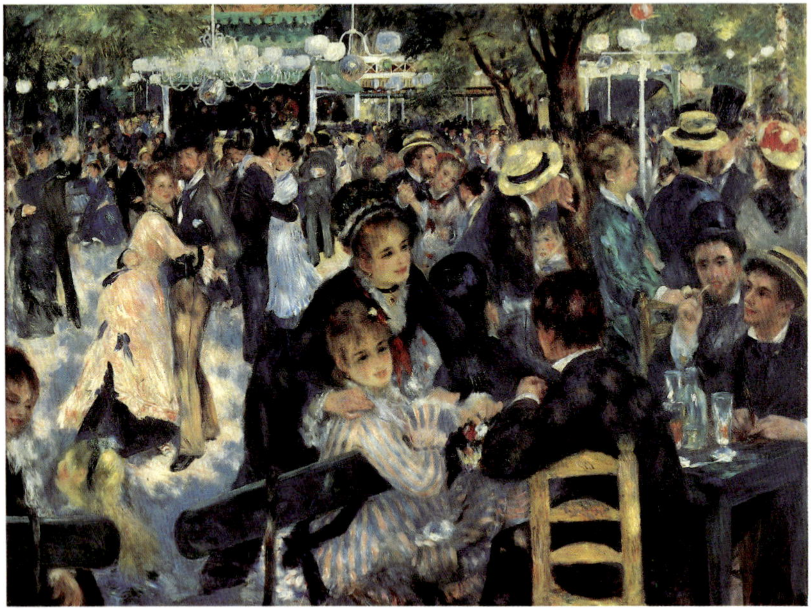

▲ **Pierre-Auguste Renoir**
Dance at the Moulin de la Galette (1876).
Oil on canvas:
131 x 175 cm.
Musée d'Orsay, Paris

What Manet's contemporaries remembered best about his great scandal-painting was the fact that he had dared to confront modern relations between men and women head on. The other Impressionists too were disinclined to pontificate about this, or to draw some kind of sociological moral from it. With commendable realism, they simply demonstrated what the nature of human relations–the "commerce" between individuals– really meant: a commerce of feminine charms in the literal sense, a power of certain men over others, and a power of certain women who (like Manet's models) seem to stare openly at those who would look at them furtively.

"Must we accept that the centre of this great city today... is an opera house? Must our future glory depend on the perfecting of our public entertainments? Is Paris no more than the capital of elegance and pleasure?"
Le Temps,
August 1867.

all the world is commerce

Until that time, portraits of women were often thinly-veiled pretexts for male licentiousness. But the domination of the male is brought to nothing when it is exposed crudely, without adornment. Today we see many of the Impressionist paintings as charming scenes, in which an attractive woman (more or less unclothed) accompanies a sober bourgeois, or in which

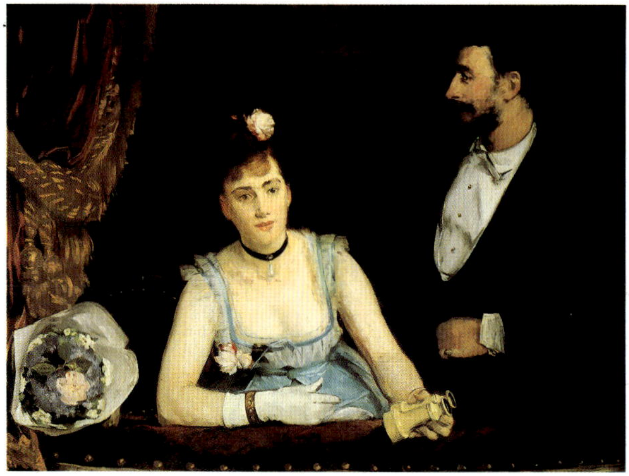

Eva Gonzalès ▶
(1849- 1883).
A box at the Italiens
(1874).
Oil on canvas:
98 x 130 cm.
Musée d'Orsay, Paris.

An impressionist by default
Eva Gonzalès, a pupil and friend of Manet, had this rendering of a favourite Impressionist theme refused by the 1874 Salon. In 1879 it was accepted, because the colours had been darkened, making it less "modern".

girls dance with students or workmen. But these were interpreted (sometimes wrongly) in the 19th century as the portrayal of a vicious milieu in which men could purchase the company of loose women, and in which prostitution was a practical means of social advancement for any girl hardy and ambitious enough to embrace the profession.
The majority of the Impressionists did not cheat about what they saw, and their work is often no more than accurately-documented real life. At the same time, they delighted in portraying a milieu which was both open and highly dubious, a milieu of which the bordello was an obvious symbol. The "modern life" they recorded was one of uncertainty, in which truth and appearances were easily confounded.

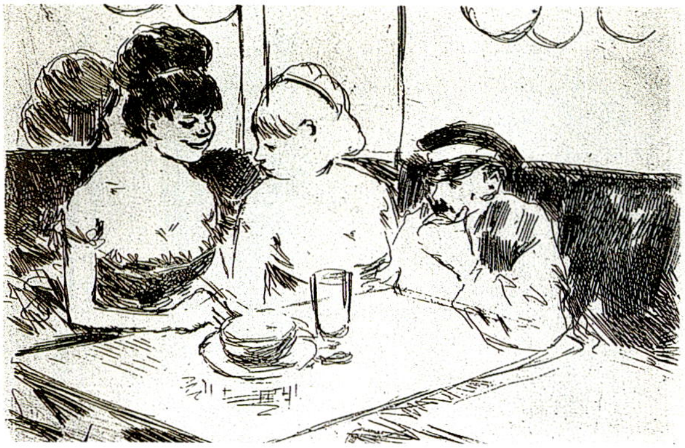

Jean-Louis Forain ▶
(1852-1931).
Brothel
(reject plate).
Etching for
J-K Huysmans'
Sketches of Paris.

"The prostitute [la fille] has found, in Forain, her truest painter."
J-K Huysmans, 1880.

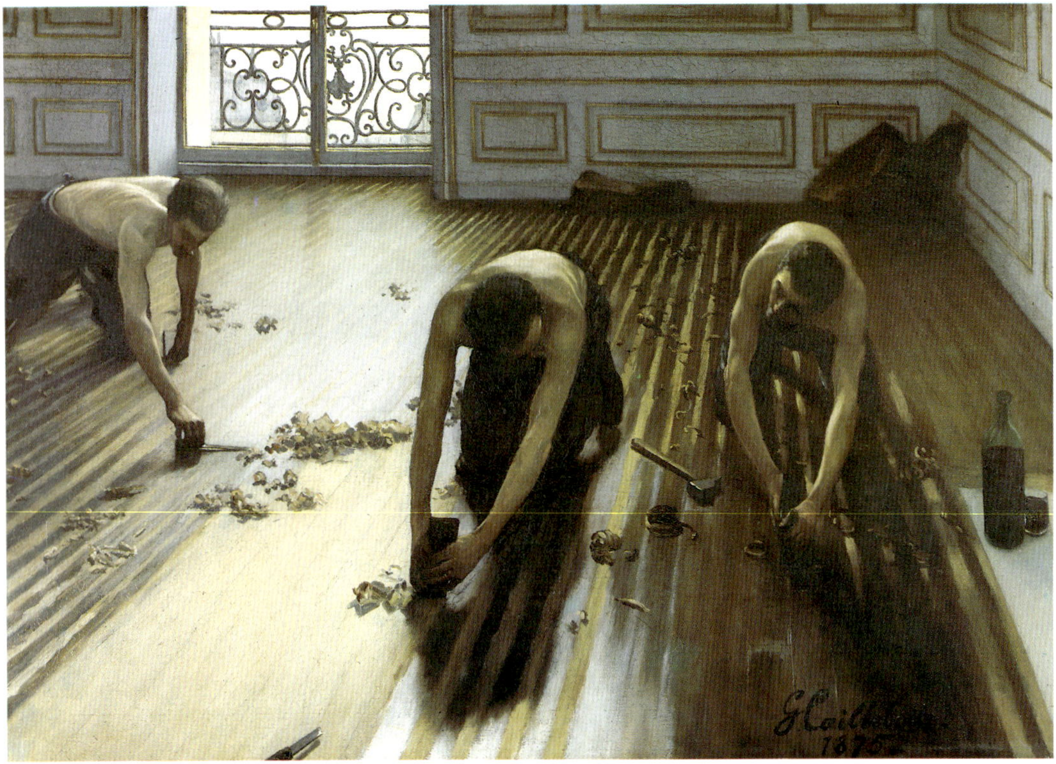

▲
Gustave Caillebotte
(1848-1894).
The Floor Planers
(1875).
Oil on canvas:
192 x 146 cm.
Musée d'Orsay, Paris.

CAILLEBOTTE

the painter and the working world

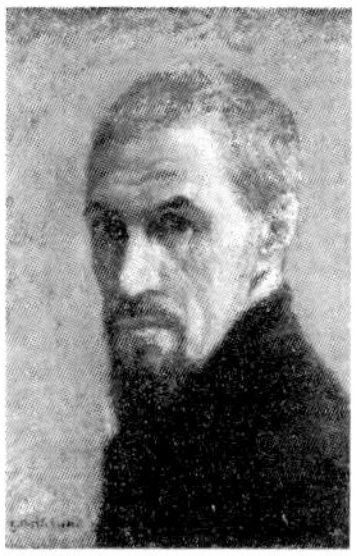

▲
Gustave Caillebotte
Self-portrait
(circa 1889), detail.
Oil on canvas:
40.5 x 32.5 cm.
Musée d'Orsay, Paris.

In this painting, men are seen at work in a modern apartment. Their professional gestures and their tools are defined with great precision, as are their clothes. There is even a bottle of wine, which the men will probably drink when their job is done. This canvas offers no moral and makes no point. It is simply a record of the world of work.

At the second Impressionist Exhibition in 1876, the subject of this painting attracted the attention of the critics who praised Caillebotte's skill–i.e. his respect for most of the academic conventions. The finished quality of the picture was admired, though the naked torsos of the workers were judged "too scrawny and pinched" and not sufficiently idealized. But the laws of perspective, correctly observed, are pushed to their limits in this painting to produce a very odd result. The scene is perceived from a very high angle, from the side. The floor is emphatically tilted, and the walls crowd in at the rear of the room. In this way our usual habits of vision are caught off guard.

Caillebotte's view
The classic perspective unites all the lines in a painting at one or two points on a horizon line, which can be higher or lower depending on the point of vantage from which the scene is envisioned.

An opportunity seized
Caillebotte did not set out to create a record of the working milieu. The apartment is typical of the new buildings constructed by Haussmann, in one of which the painter resided. It may even be that these floor planers were working in his own home.

an impartial view of manual labour

To depict this scene from life, Caillebotte carefully sketched his workers' gestures. Their poses give a clear idea of the physical effort they are expending, and in portraying them Caillebotte offered a completely fresh view of work, without a hint of superiority.

the impartial eye

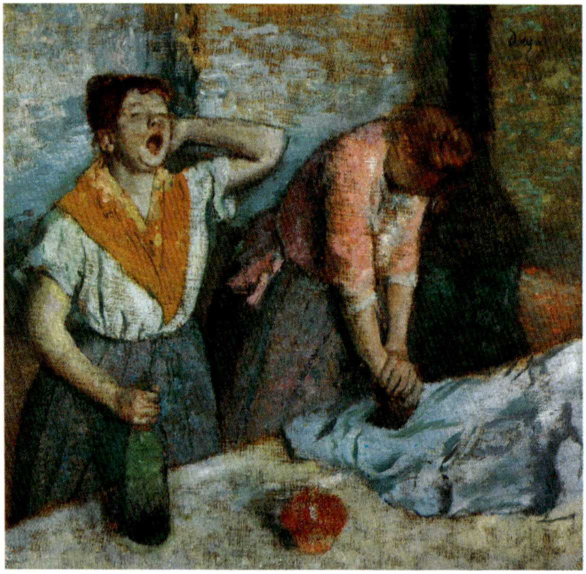

◄ **Edgar Degas**
Women Ironing
(about 1884).
Oil on canvas:
76 x 81 cm.
Musée d'Orsay, Paris.

"It is one thing to paint laundresses moving in decorative shadows, as Teniers did; it is quite another to show them yawning over an ironing table."
G. Moore, 1890.

Certain Impressionists seem to have assumed the task of painting the world of work, currently being examined in such novels as Zola's *Les Rougon-Macart* and in the works of the Goncourt brothers. While the more famous Impressionist paintings describe a world of leisure, there are many more whose themes are less agreeable.

On occasion, this presentation took on a denunciatory character, as in the paintings of the anarchist Pissarro. But this was infrequent, and Pissarro himself usually confined his paintings to the harmless activities of country folk. At the same time, Degas was beginning to register a certain disgust for some of the things he saw. Yet in most cases the painter's eye remained neutral and detached; its concern was to show the reality of modern working life as effectively as possible.

For example, they lavished enormous care on the material details of work, from manual craftsmanship to international commerce and finance. The specific objects and gestures of each profession were mi nutely studied and transcribed.

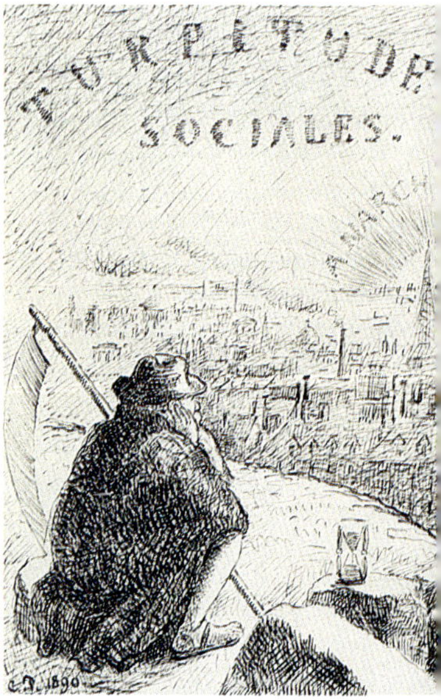

Camille Pissarro ►
Social Turpitudes
(1890).
Cover of an album of 28 drawings in brown ink, on smooth-glazed paper:
31.5 x 24.5 cm.
Skira Collection, Switzerland.

Even the lives of people who lived on unearned income, a common condition among the French bourgeoisie to which most of the Impressionists belonged, were described in terms of stock exchange sessions, strolls in parks and streets, and café scenes, in which less respectable professionals (waitresses, prostitutes, singers) made their appearance.

The Anarchist Impressionist
The Impressionists held widely different political views. The most consistent among them was Pissarro, a lifelong anarchist who rejected bourgeois values and institutions out of hand. Even his rural paintings seem to yearn for an ideological "age of harmony".

a depersonalised world

The men and women who made up this society had hitherto been ignored by the arts. They are shown to be uniformly absorbed by their occupations. In Impressionist scenes showing larger numbers of figures, each one seems to be linked with the others purely within the framework of their strictly professional relationships. Basically society is portrayed as a collection of individual workers without individuality.

Edgar Degas
The Cotton Exchange
(New Orleans),
(1873).
Oil on canvas:
73 x 92 cm.
Musée des Beaux Arts,
Pau.

Here Degas shows a scene at the Louisiana Cotton Exchange. The only people in it who are idle happen to be his two brothers.

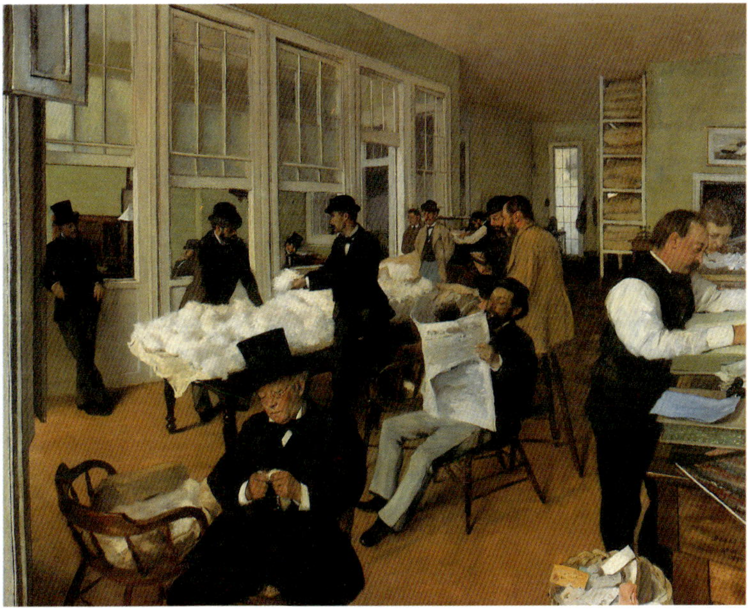

the theme of work in art

Renoir was the only one for whom modern work conditions presented no interest. He was nostalgic for a rural, artisan-dominated society. As the son of a porcelain worker, his ideal was the era of Louis XV, when (so he believed) no work was ever sordid or trying. With the exception of Renoir, no other Impressionist completely neglected work as a crucial aspect of everyday life; probably because the industrialization of France was everywhere obvious, having made huge advances in the reign of Louis-Philippe before coming fully into its own under Napoleon III. This is why so many Impressionist works are enlivened by hurrying crowds of the less-than-wealthy.

Labourer's work, artist's work
Here Monet makes a distinction between three aspects of modern life, which also apply to the work of the artist. The work itself is a uniform thing, insignificant compared to the end product. The repetition of identical gestures–carrying coal-sacks or applying brushstrokes–is at the root of work. The result is in itself a spectacle, for loafers and museum browsers.

the representation of work in all its forms

In the case of Monet, who was otherwise so little inclined to paint the drearier aspects of life, there is one canvas in particular–*The Coal Heavers*–in which work is taken as a valid topic for art. Here Monet does not dwell on the physical efforts of his subjects; he seems more intrigued by their rigorous organization and by

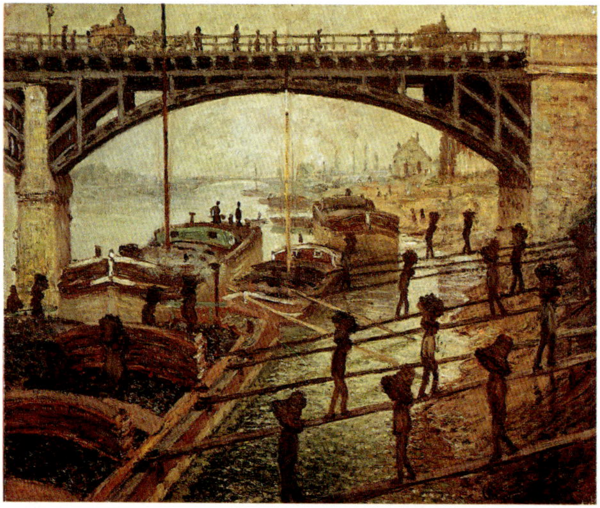

◄ **Claude Monet**
The Coal Heavers
(1875).
Oil on canvas:
54 x 64.8 cm.
Durand-Ruel
Collection, Paris.

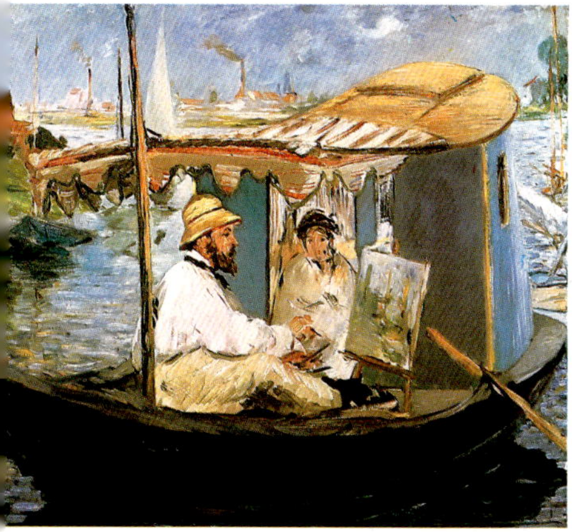

◄ **Edouard Manet**
Claude Monet and his wife in his floating studio (1874).
Oil on canvas:
82.5 x 105 cm.
Neue Pinakothek,
Munich.

At Argenteuil, near the factories, the Impressionist painter was also hard at work.

more intrigued by their rigorous organization and by the regularity of their movements. As with his Impressionist colleagues, work is primarily what creates original effects. It is also given an aesthetic dimension: many Impressionist paintings expressly include the idlers who invariably stand about watching others at work. This aesthetic approach also leads to studies of atmospheres that are more directly characteristic of Impressionism. For example modern machinery furnishes a type of smoke which is rare in nature, but produced in abundance by industry, with its belching chimneys and furnaces.
As to the professional category of work to which the painters themselves belonged, this was in no way neglected. The subject was not original, since from the earliest times painters had portrayed themselves at their easels, brush in hand. By contrast the Impressionists presented themselves as ordinary workers functioning midway between work and leisure.

Camille Pissarro ►
The Great Bridge of Rouen (1896).
Oil on canvas:
65.5 x 92 cm.
Carnegie Institute,
Pittsburgh,
Pennsylvania.

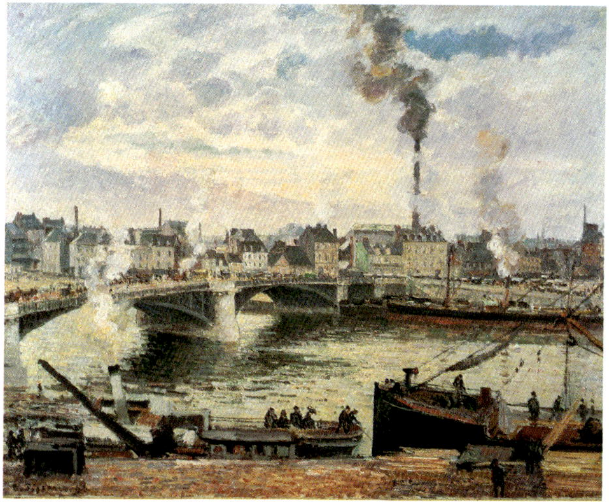

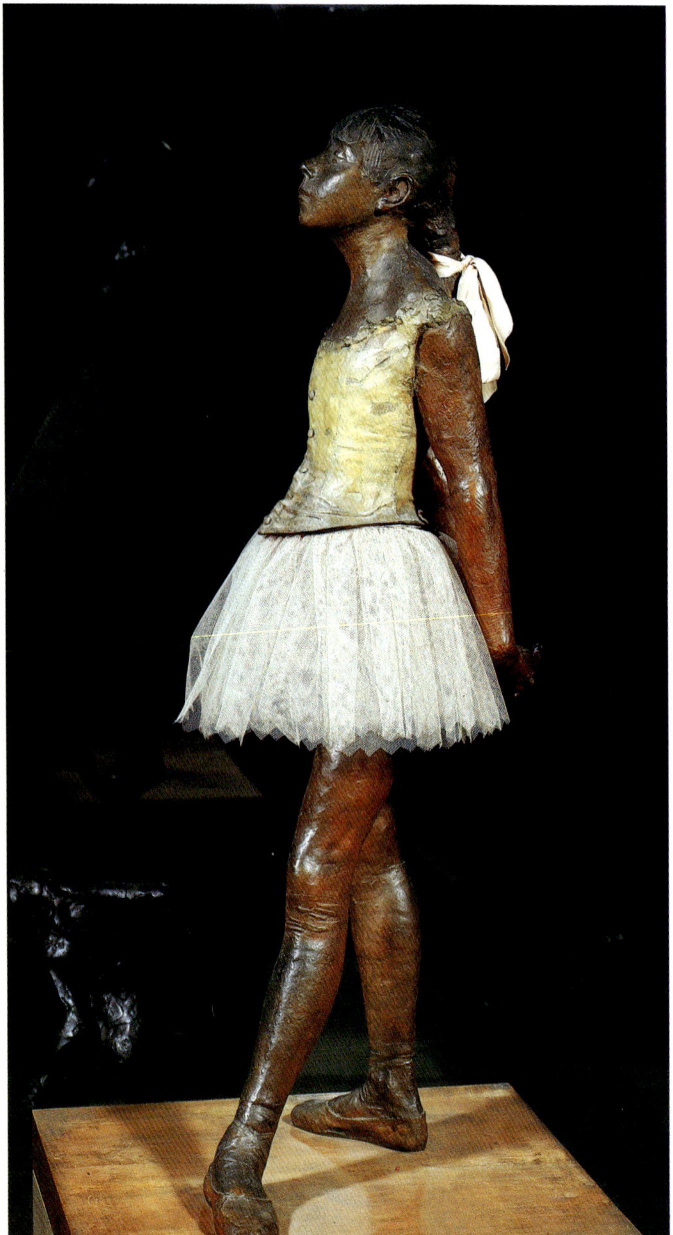

EDGAR DEGAS

society's mirror

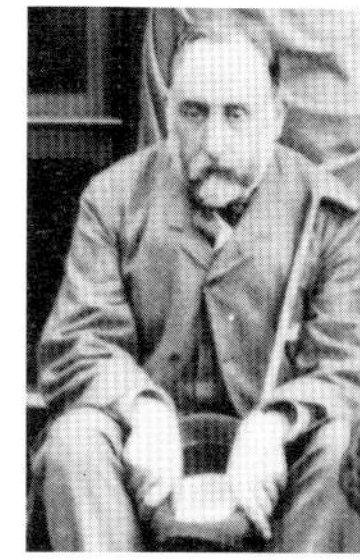

▲ *Apotheosis of Degas* (1885),.detail. Photograph by Barnes. Bibliothèque Nationale, Paris.

A small bronze statue, dressed in fabric like an outsize doll. If you look at this figure cursorily, you may conclude that it is merely a charming piece, the faithful likeness of a teenage girl in a tutu gracefully executing the fourth position. But if you look closer, you realize that something unsettling emanates from the piece.

The impression of naturalism is dominant here. The movement of the ballerina has been carefully studied, in dozens of preliminary sketches and sculptures of the same model in the nude. Her name is known to us: she was Marie Van Goethem, born in 1864, a dancer at the opera. With great finesse, Degas has modelled all the anatomical characteristics of his ballerina. But he has also left traces of his own handiwork, those tiny irregularities which give more life to a work of art than mechanical precision ever could.

"M. Degas has exhibited... next to his arresting studies of criminals in courtrooms, a wax ballerina of a naturalism which is oddly attractive... the vicious, guttersnipe mask of this pubescent girl is unforgettable." J. Claretie, 1884.

a disturbing face

What is shocking here is the face. Thrust backward, with receding forehead and simian jawline, it borders on caricature. Degas has clearly set out to represent a whole social group through this one individual. He was inspired by the theories of physiognomy, a doctrine which suggests that the exterior aspects of people make it possible to pinpoint their characters, moral qualities and social status. And everything about this ballerina leads us to conclude that she was a typical example of a dancer of humble origin condemned to a life of vice. In short, for Degas she is an object of scientific interest.

◄ **Edgar Degas** (1834-1917). *14-year-old Ballerina* (1879-1881). Bronze, partially tinted, cotton skirt, satin ribbon, wooden base: height 95.2 cm. Musée d'Orsay, Paris.

Degas and the mask of corruption

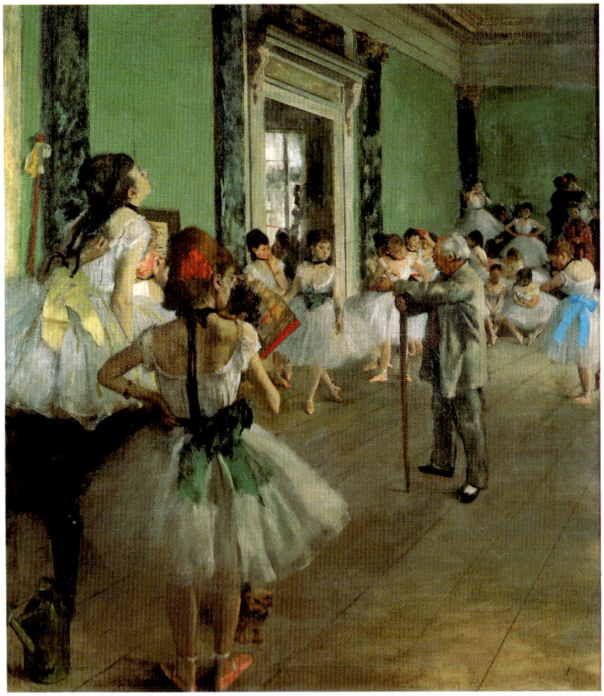

◄ **Edgar Degas**
The Dancing Class
(1873-1876).
Oil on canvas:
85x 75 cm.
Musée d'Orsay, Paris.

In the early 1870's, Degas invoked the inventor of physiognomy when outlining his plan for "a study of modern sentiment", whereby he would describe in his works "the habits of a race". He believed in the quasi-scientific possibilities of art in the domain of sociology, and apparently decided to conduct a systematic exploration of certain categories of the population, along with certain places. Among these was the Paris Opera, a building he had frequented for many years, which proved to be a fertile ground for observation. This interest was quite a trend, given that at the same time Degas' best friend Ludovic Halévy published a series of satirical stories, *La Famille Cardinal*, which recounted the

Physiognomy
Invented by Lavater in the late 18th century, this pseudo-science was very popular in the 19th century. Writers (notably Balzac), artists and criminologists of the period were ardent subscribers to it.

Edgar Degas
The café-concert singer Theresa performing the "dog song".
Leaf from a notebook, 1877.
▼

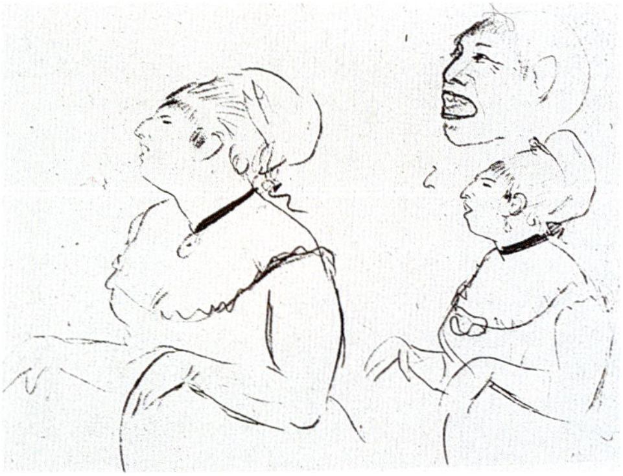

adventures of two young ballerinas at the Opera. Degas based a series of monotypes on this work.
Degas was not satisfied merely to offer a typology of faces suggesting (with no further explanation) a sordid reality beneath a brilliant surface. He faithfully recorded gestures and attitudes. He reproduced all the important features in the world of a dancer: the lessons, exercises, rehearsals, performances, boxes and backstage life. With his elusive perspectives, and technique–he used either pastel, a medium felt to be ephemeral in its very nature, or transparent oils–he suggested the fickleness of the world. His ballerinas show how an uncouth working girl can change into a stage star. Or vice versa.

"Degas' attitude to these little creatures, and theirs toward him, was very droll. He found them charming, and treated them like his own children... they venerated him in return, and the smallest slip of a girl would give whatever she could to please Degas."
D. Halévy, 1891

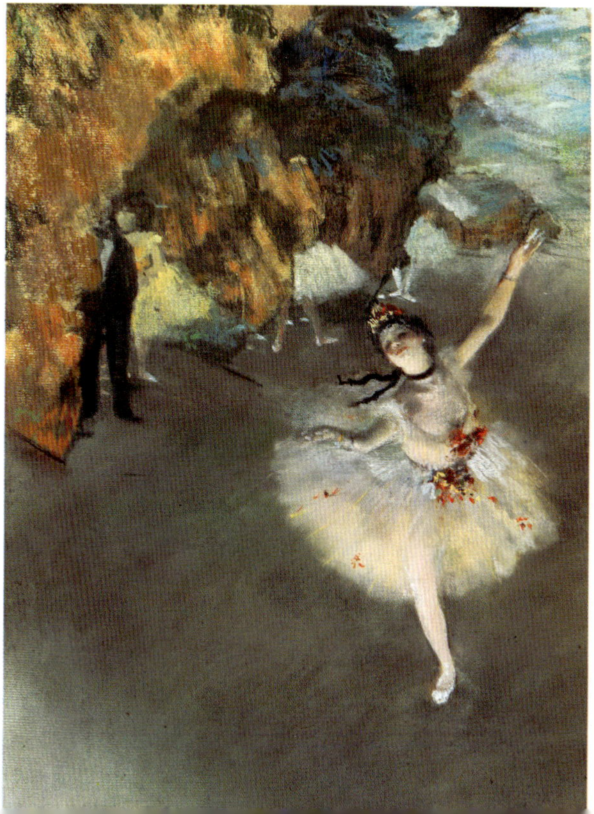

◄ **Edgar Degas**
Ballet, also called
The Star
(1876-1877).
Pastel on monotype:
58 x 42 cm.
Musée d'Orsay, Paris.

the captured instant

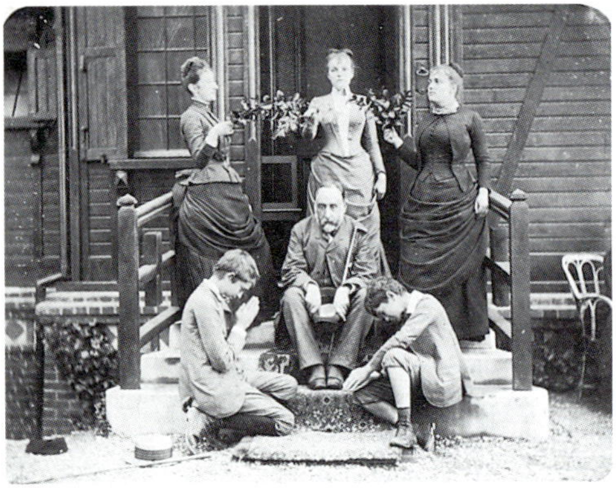

▲ *Apotheosis of Degas* (parody of *the Apotheosis of Homer*, by Ingres) (1885). Photograph. Bibliothèque Nationale, Paris.

While staying with friends, Degas posed for this joke photograph.

Degas was an Impressionist in the sense that he set out to illustrate fleeting sensations which had previously been dismissed as inartistic. But above all he was a realist who wanted to achieve in painting what Balzac, Zola and the Goncourts had achieved in literature, namely to "capture, by copying modern life, the soul within that life". He was not interested in reproducing the superficial aspects of what he saw–for that, photography was better adapted. Instead he injected his own life and way of perceiving things into his work; like Manet before him, he painted ordinary items, but used them to reflect more general characteristics. Degas paid close attention to the details of the present, but also to the place of his work in art history. In other words he dealt with exterior subjects, but showed their aesthetic qualities to advantage.

Degas' ambition for his art knew no bounds, which is why his works can be "read" on many different levels.

Edgar Degas ▶
Robert le Diable's Ballet (1876).
Oil on canvas: 76.6 x 81.3 cm.
Victoria and Albert Museum, London.

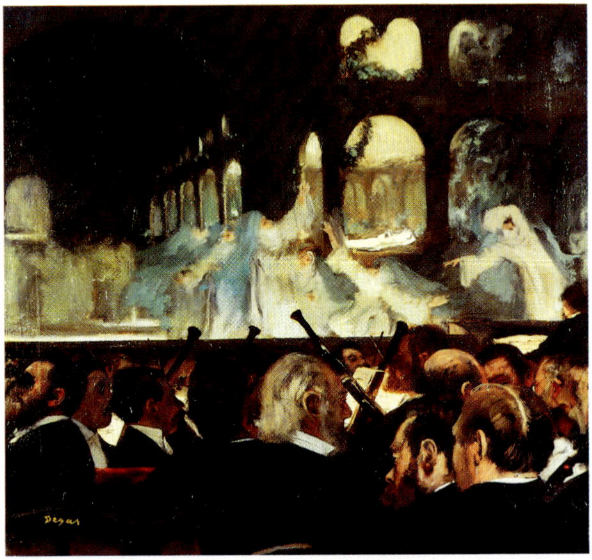

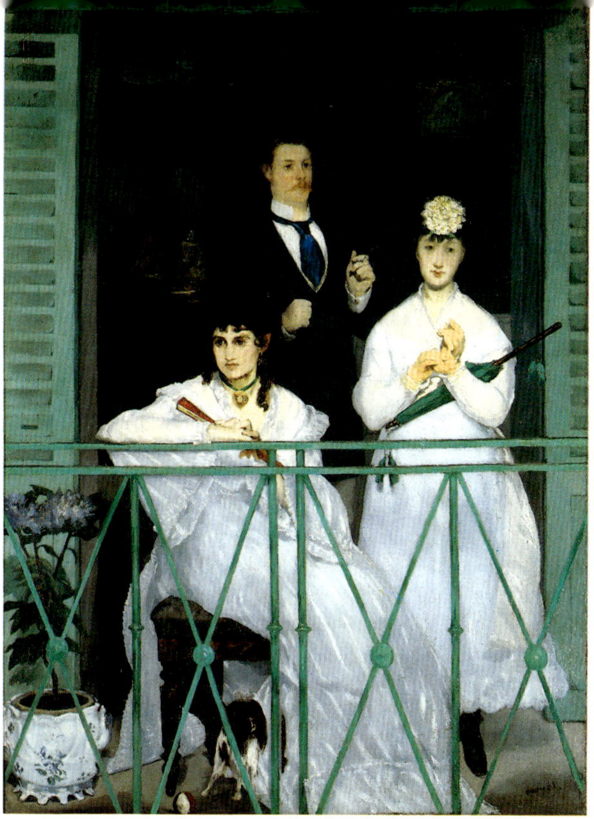

◄ **Edouard Manet**
The Balcony
(1868-1869).
Oil on canvas:
169 x 125 cm.
Musée d'Orsay, Paris.

In *The Balcony*, Manet painted three of his friends with a child. Berthe Morisot (seated) found her portrait "strange". Manet emphasized and isolated the characters, probably to underline the modernity of a scene which nonetheless had many precursors in the history of art.

Image-framing and photography
It is generally thought that the Impressionists' unusual framing of their images aped photography. In reality, photography with its long exposures made meticulous composition essential: only painting, by contrast, could impart a sense of spontaneity and immediacy.

He wrote that he wanted to be the "classical painter of modern life". Ingres was his model, because alone in the 19th century Ingres had preserved the tradition of painting for eternity by the strength of his composition and draftsmanship. Degas composed his own pictures with equal care.

organizing spontaneity

Nevertheless Degas' paintings are arranged with a view to communicating a sense of spontaneity, as though the scene had been viewed on the sly, or framed at random. Each plane of the picture is taken in turn, as if the eye were moving from one vantage point to the next, passing from the audience to the stage without a pause. It lingers on feature after feature, analysing the anecdotes, the portraits, the patterns, and the pictural devices employed by Degas, who was the supreme master of a genre he invented himself.

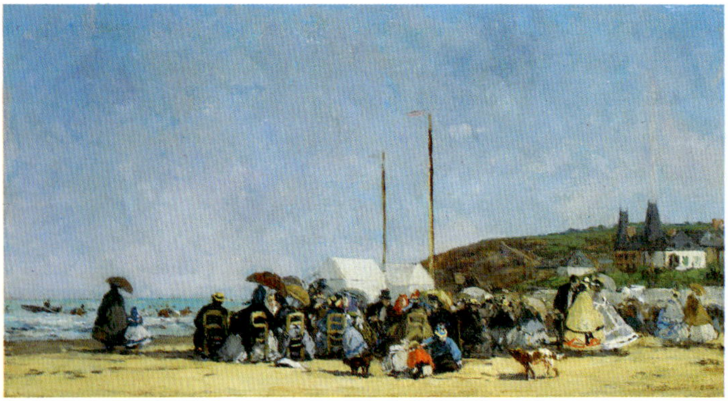

Claude Monet
Terrace at Sainte-Adresse
(1867).
Oil on canvas:
98 x 130 cm.
Metropolitan Museum of Art,
New York.
▼

▲ **Eugène Boudin**
(1824-1898).
The Beach at Trouville
(1864).
Oil on canvas:
26 x 48 cm.
Musée d'Orsay, Paris.

Corot called Boudin "the prince of skies". He began painting the coast near Honfleur at an early stage, producing views in which the clouds are balanced by groups of holiday-makers. Boudin's urge to paint nature "in all her variety and freshness", as well as the advice he gave to the young Monet, made him one of the forerunners of Impressionism.

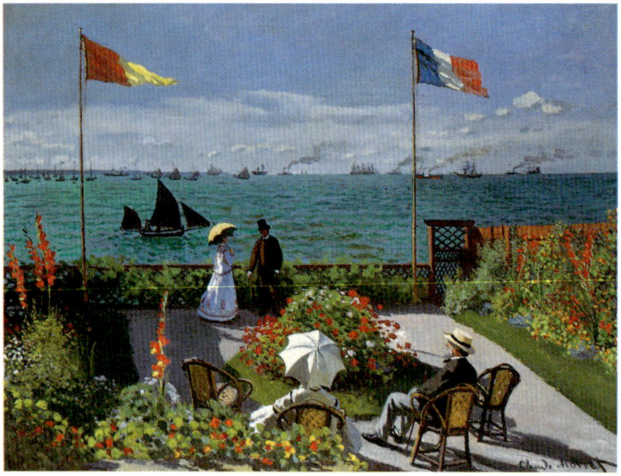

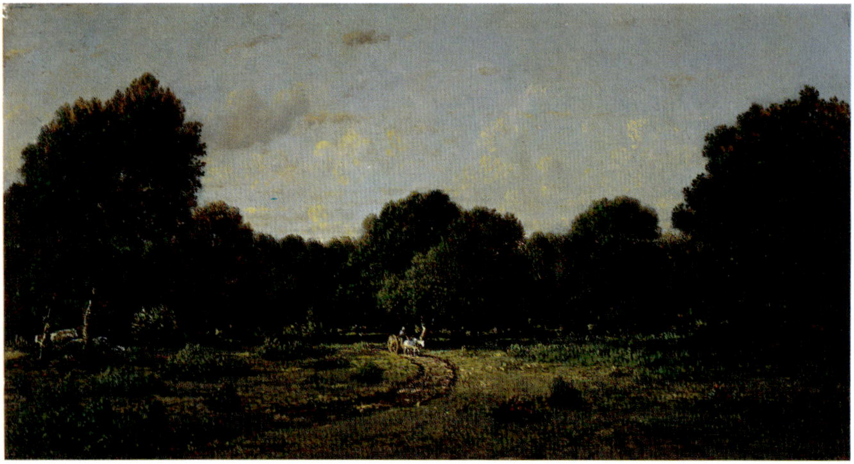

◄ **Théodore Rousseau**
(1812-1867).
Forest Clearing, also called *The Wagon*
(1863).
Oil on canvas:
28 x 53 cm.
Musée d'Orsay, Paris.

In the 1840's, Rousseau was one of the masters of the Barbizon school, a group of painters who sought to paint direct from nature.

Pioneers of landscape art

After 1845, the critics were persuaded that Corot and Rousseau, the leaders of the Barbizon School, had succeeded in renewing landscape art by giving it greater realism–and by concentrating on the ordinary French countryside, previously neglected. One of their most brilliant disciples was Eugène Boudin, the painter of the restless skies of Normandy.
As a young man, Monet met Boudin at Le Havre in 1858. He worked beside him for several seasons and was later a firm believer in the older man's theory that artists should work in the open air, in the places they were trying to paint, and scrupulously reproduce what they saw. Together the two painters moved up and down the Channel coast looking for subject matter, producing work which expressed their interest not only in the picturesque qualities of places and people, but also in the specific atmospheric conditions in each place. Previously, artists confined their exterior work to studies, and their final versions were painted in the studio. The perfecting of portable easels, and of oil paints in tubes which could be carried about without drying, now made it possible to do all the work outside.

Monet transmitted this open air theory to his Paris friends, who took it up enthusiastically and began to travel around the countryside, in the wake of the growing fashion for tourism. Their first major themes were the French coastline and the suburbs of Paris.
In the 1870's, the cityscape was added, as a theme, to the country landscape favoured by earlier generations of artists. Country landscapes were often enlivened by figures and buildings; city-scapes invariably so. It was not so much the urban monuments which interested the Impressionists, as the agitation of modern towns, with their crowds, their new forms of transport, and their specific atmospheres.

Pierre-Auguste Renoir
The Mosque (Arab festival) (1881).
Oil on canvas:
73 x 92 cm.
Musée d'Orsay, Paris.

Renoir concentrated on the Ile-de-France and the South. This "local colour" painting, done during a visit to Algeria, is an exception in his work. ►

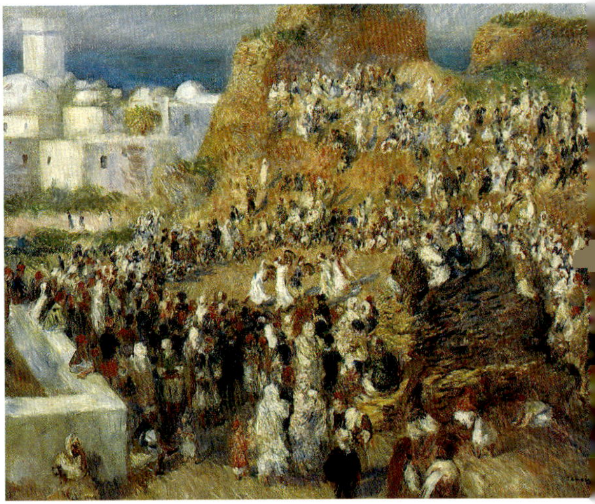

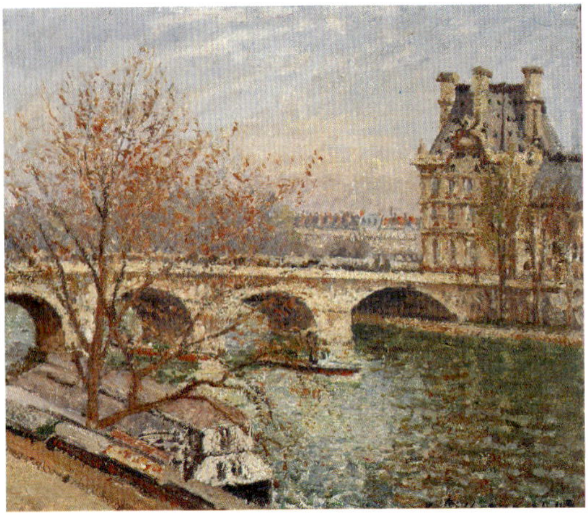

▲
Camille Pissarro
The Pont Royal and the Pavillon de Flore
(1903).
Oil on canvas:
54.5 x 65 cm.
Musée du Petit Palais, Paris.

In his final year, Pissarro painted views of Paris and Le Havre. Here, he blends nature (the sky, the tree and the river) with the modern cityscape (buildings along the Rue de Rivoli, river barges) with a paramount symbol of artistic glory: the Louvre.

Paul Cézanne
The Montagne Sainte Victoire
(1890-1894).
Oil on canvas:
54.6 x 64.8 cm.
National Gallery of Scotland, Edinburgh.
▼

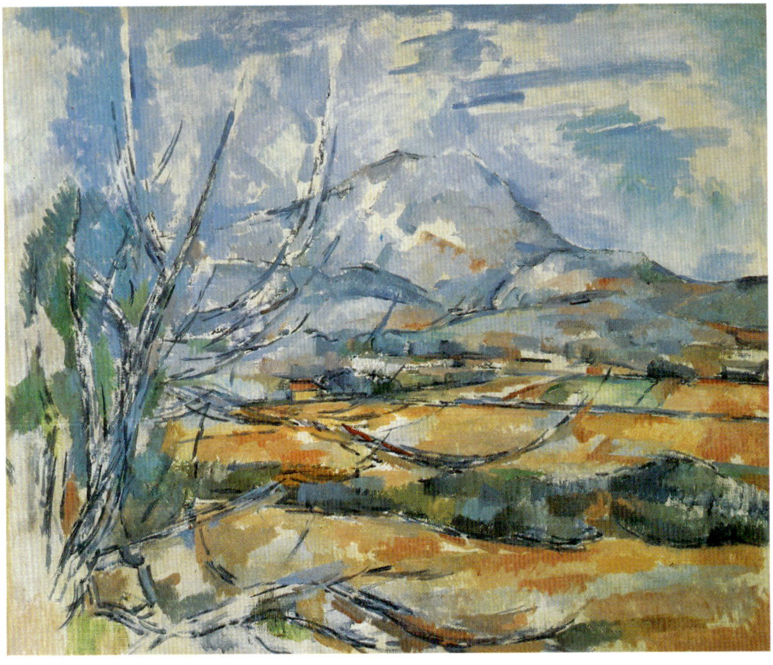

Thus the Impressionists explored the French landscape. They refused to fall back on conventional composition and often adopted eccentric approaches that laid no special emphasis on any one element at the expense of the rest. In addition, the techniques they used placed objects and the air surrounding them on the same plane of importance.

When, in 1880, Impressionists grew tired of constantly looking for new "typical" places, they did not wholly abandon open air work. For Renoir and Monet, the landscape emerged as a vehicle for the play of light and atmosphere. To achieve the widest possible variety of effects, they slowed down the frequency of their travels, searched abroad for the picturesque subjects they now rejected in France, and finally undertook in-depth studies of a very few motifs–Cagnes and the Nice region in the case of Renoir, and Giverny in the case of Monet. Pissarro and Cézanne did much the same, restricting themselves respectively to Pontoise and Aix-en-Provence, which they investigated tirelessly for over twenty years until they had extracted their natural essence.

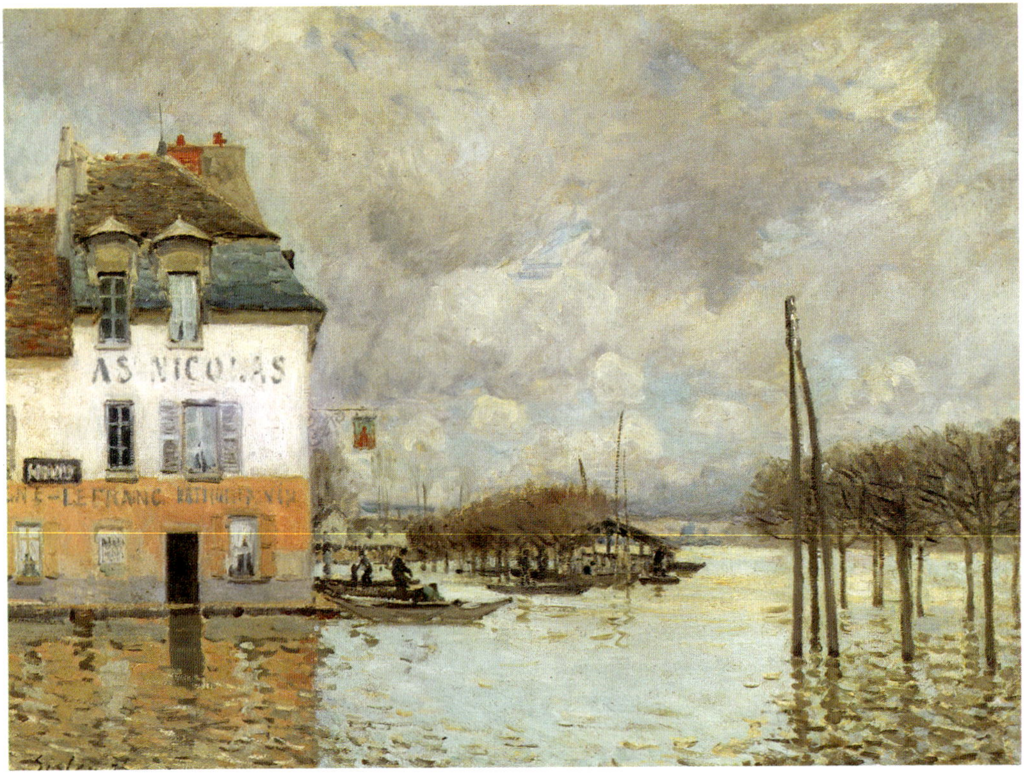

▲

Alfred Sisley
(1839-1899).
Flooding at Port-Marly (1876).
Oil on canvas:
60 x 81 cm.
Musée d'Orsay, Paris.

ALFRED SISLEY

the harmonies of places

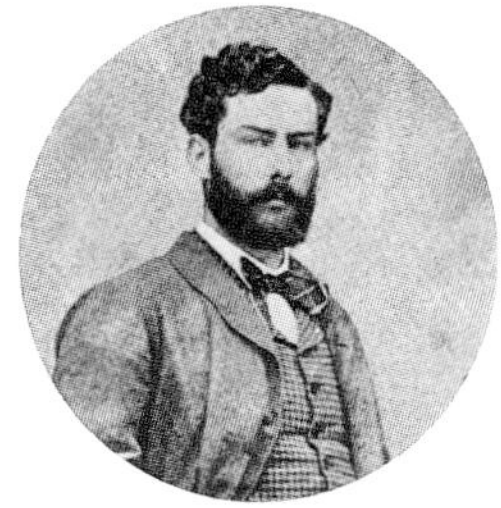

▲
Alfred Sisley.
Photograph.

The Saint-Germain crossroads is invaded by the flood waters of the Seine. Water, earth and sky are blended into one. With its multitude of firm, rapid brushstrokes, this Paris suburban landscape brings together urban architecture and rural vegetation. Despite the bad weather and the threatening dark clouds, the canvas seems to exhale a sense of peace and harmony.

One of many canvases
Sisley painted several canvases on this subject, in 1872 and later in 1876, at which time he did six views of the Seine in flood, mostly from an identical point of vantage. He also painted Port Marly and its surroundings at more ordinary times, with a marked preference for serene atmospherics.

The storm theme, which was a particular favorite with the English painter Alfred Sisley, recurs throughout the history of European art. As a general rule the storm is taken as a symbol for the inner conflict of the figures in the paintings, or else as an indication of some universal tragedy. By contrast, Sisley's flood scenes convey tranquillity, absence of drama, pathos. Drifting onward from the spectacle of the boats and the river landing-stage under the chestnut trees, the eye of the observer moves without interruption to the long, low line of the horizon, before continuing to the right along a calm diagonal.

A classical composition
Sisley's composition here is a balance between the closed, architectural surface at left, and the more open vegetation at right.

the harmony of nature

This impression of harmony is accentuated by the dominant grey-blue, which absorbs one or two red and ochre spots in the building and in its reflection. Even though details (such as the St Nicolas wineshop) are fairly numerous, they all recede into the general landscape, which is a vehicle for recording changing weather conditions rather than a picturesque subject in itself.

A horror of the pictu-resque

Alfred Sisley was probably the most conventional of the Impressionists. His determination to paint landscapes made him a typical member of the group, and perhaps the only one who was undeviating in his loyalty to naturalism, the faithful transcription of nature. He was also alone in continuing to work entirely in the open air and from life. His landscapes of the Ile-de-France, from Poissy to Moret-sur-Loing, gave meaning to the most mundane French countryside; he did not seek out the picturesque for its own sake in France, any more than he did in his views of London and Cardiff suburbs.

A far remove from Romanticism
The Impressionists to some extent carried on the tradition of landscape painting, while rejecting subjects whose wildness might provoke deeper contemplation. They also avoided places that were charged with symbolism, until about 1880 when their acknowledged mastery gave them licence to use grand and historic places.

the fleeting quality of nature

Sisley seems to have deliberately chosen subjects which would allow him to stay in touch with the shifting spectacle of nature, while retaining a certain stability of composition. His friends were more inclined to paint their landscapes without any special rigour. The

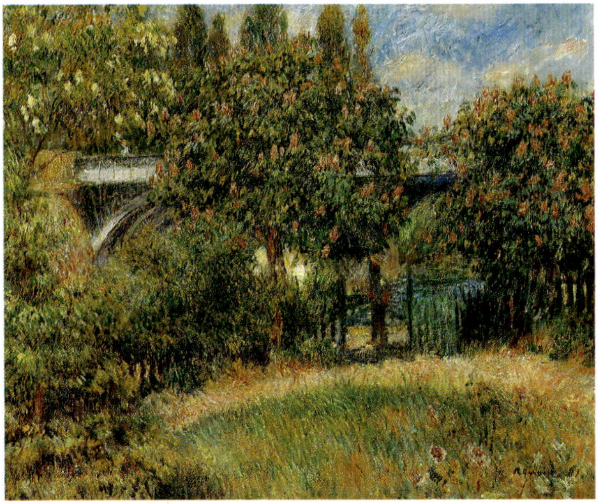

Pierre-Auguste Renoir ▶
The Railway Bridge at Chatou (1881).
Oil on canvas:
54 x 65.5 cm.
Museée d'Orsay, Paris.

For Renoir, the presence of nature absorbs everything else. Even this piece of industrial construction is lost in a garden's vegetation.

Neo-Impressionism, or Divisionism
In 1884, the young Seurat's *Bathing at Asnières* placed Neo-Impressionism squarely in the forefront of art. He pursued the Impressionist interest in light in a scientific way. His colours were no longer mixed on his palette, merely juxtaposed on canvas to create an "optical blend".

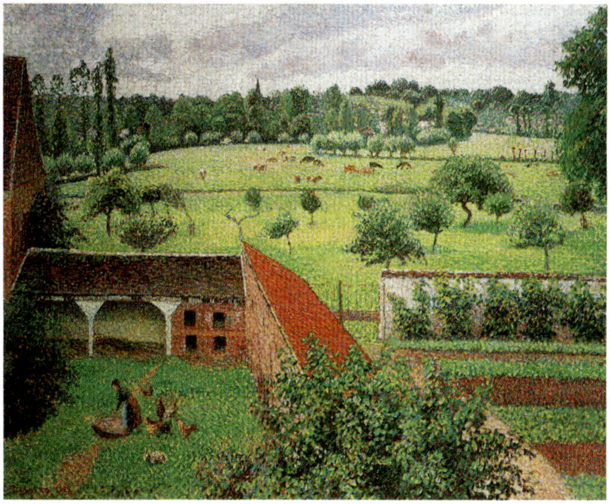

◄ **Camille Pissarro**
View from my window, Eragny-sur-Epte (1886-1888).
Oil on canvas: 65 x 80 cm.
Ashmolean Museum, Oxford.

Pissarro, by then an old man, was galvanized by his meeting with Seurat. Between 1886 and 1890 he became a vociferous convert to Neo-Impressionism, before reverting to a more flexible approach.

subject would be chosen at random, on a walk (say) through fields and villages–as if the artist had halted just here because it was a place where he could set up his easel without trouble and stay until his painting session was over. Thus the composition tends to be either uncentred, or else deliberately monotonous.
Impressionist landscapes generally contain people: or at least they show traces of human presence. They are never thick forests, majestic mountains, or austere deserts. Instead they depict arable fields, and segments of nature containing human figures and habitations.

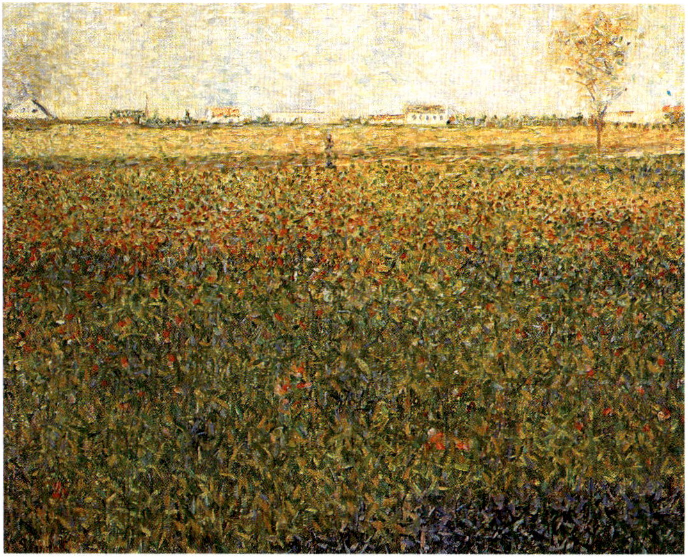

◄ **Georges Seurat** (1859-1891).
Field of lucerne at Saint-Denis (1885).
Oil on canvas: 65 x 81 cm.
National Gallery of Scotland, Edinburgh.

The regularity of this suburban backwater upstages the small factory, above left.

the benefits of progress

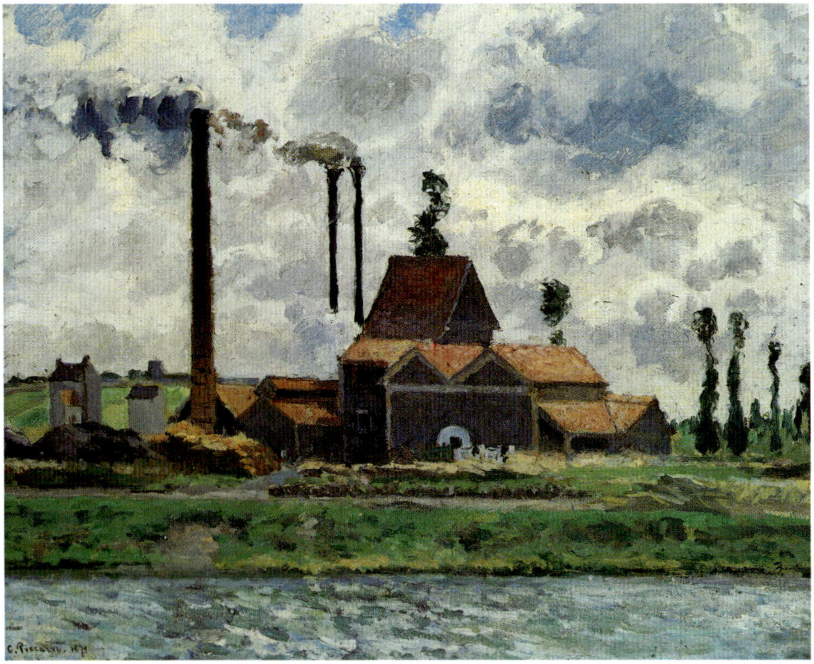

▲
Camille Pissarro
Factory near Pontoise (1873).
Oil on canvas: 47.7 x 55.9 cm.
Museum of Fine Arts, Springfield.

After 1872, Pissarro became interested in the modernization of the Pontoise landscape surrounding his home. Here, a monument-like factory is the central motif of a richly-nuanced scene.

The Impressionist landscape is in many ways composed of segments of ordinary nature, which we contemplate today with nostalgia but which at the time seemed thoroughly insignificant. Anything could be a pretext for painting, and the word "nature" assumed a broader sense than before, coming to mean everything that exists at a given moment. All places were considered equivalent, and were treated as backdrops for changing effects of light, air, etc. The painted space became that which gave material value to the passage of time and the seasons.

The suburbs
The outer suburbs of Paris, where town met country, could be easily reached by train. They were much favoured by the Impressionists in the 1870's.

the industrialized landscape

To paint places is to capture the transformations that the weather operates upon them. It is also to reproduce the particularities of the era in which the scene is captured. In a very important sense, the transformations the countryside was undergoing were recorded by the Impressionists, who not infrequently gave pride of place to the superficial elements of modernity: factories, railway bridges, steel structures. The artists them-

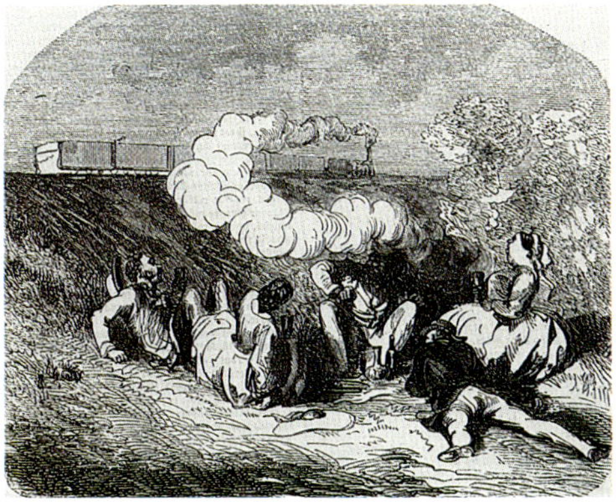

selves benefitted from technical progress, which allowed them to vary their motifs by moving rapidly from one place to another. The development of the railways, which made touring easier and created a broad suburban band around Paris, also made it possible for artists to practice a kind of pictural tourism vis-à-vis the French countryside, while staying in touch with the capital from which they came. Technological innovation appeared over and over again in their subject matter. While the elements of industry were bypassed by such artists as Renoir and Sisley, for whom landscapes expressed a certain nostalgia for a world that existed prior to the 19th-century revolutions, they were fully embraced by Monet and Pissarro, who knew they were carrying revolution into the core of art itself.

◀ **Gustave Doré** (1832-1883). *Country amusements at the Parc du Vésinet.* Engraving from *Histoire des Environs du Nouveau Paris*, by E. de la Bédollière (1861).

Claude Monet ▶
The Railway Bridge, Argenteuil (1873-1874).
Oil on canvas: 55 x 72 cm.
Musée d'Orsay, Paris.

Here industry, with its trains and viaducts, encroaches on the peace of the suburbs.

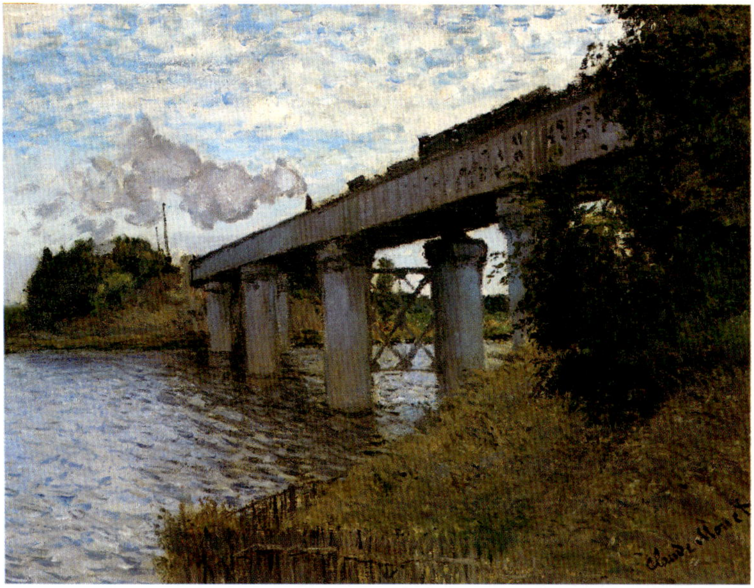

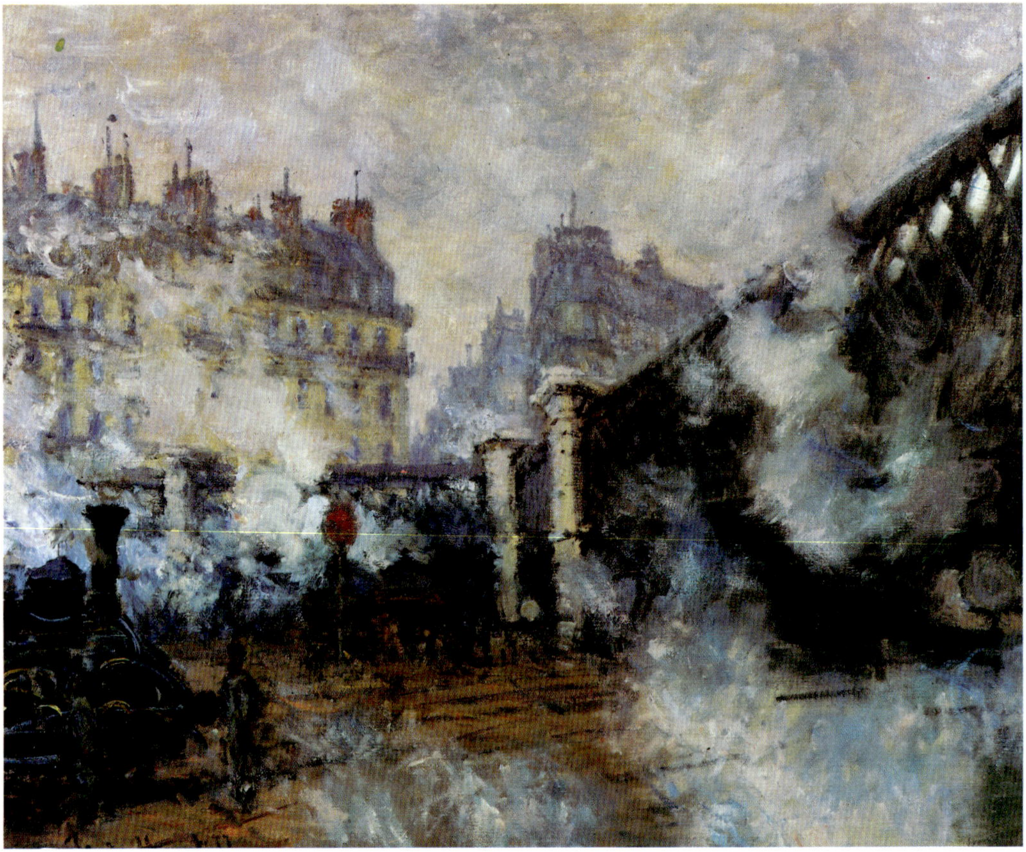

▲

Claude Monet
(1840-1926).
The Gare Saint-Lazare and the Pont de l'Europe (1877).
Oil on canvas:
64 x 81 cm.
Musée Marmottan, Paris.

CLAUDE MONET

the energy of modern cities

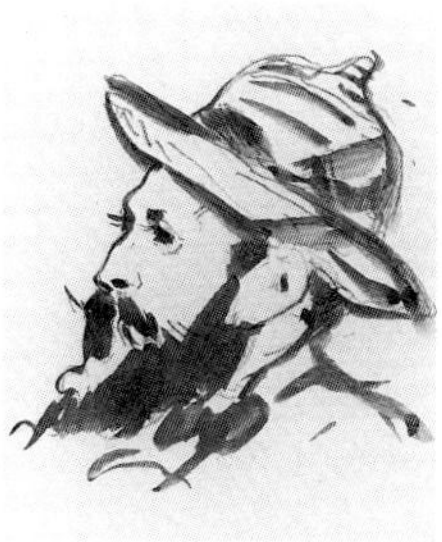

▲
Edouard Manet
Claude Monet
(about 1874).
Ink wash:
17 x 13.5 cm.
Musée Marmottan,
Paris.

A locomotive, railway tracks, a steel bridge, recently constructed buildings–strange subject matter for a painting. Nevertheless, this scene captured Monet's interest, who painted seven versions of it in early 1877 and chose to exhibit all of them at the Third Impressionist Exhibition in March of the same year.

Monet varied his position from one canvas to the next, sometimes placing himself on the inside of the station, and sometimes on the outside, at times laying his emphasis on the machines and at times on the urban landscape. This version is the one in which the point of vantage is least centred, and which offers the greatest degree of equilibrium between the two principal elements. Like Caillebotte and Manet before him, Monet turned the Gare Saint-Lazare into a primary, even symbolic element of the great modern city.

Fragments of the cityscape
Monet depicts neither the inhabitants of the quarter–the bourgeois whom his friends painted–nor the broad perspectives revealed by Haussmann's new avenues. He is content to give us a passing glimpse of recently-erected buildings, which converge on the composition's centre.

the station and the city

Again like Caillebotte and Manet, he painted the *quartier* in which he lived, newly built by Haussmann, which was typical of the gigantic planning changes then under way in Paris. For Monet the essence of a city lay in its agitation, or rather in the way the prevailing light gave harmony to disparity and dissonance. The architecture, the workers, the machines and the smoke were together a part of this peculiarly urban atmosphere, which is rendered with swirling, elegantly-intersecting brushstrokes.

Monet's urban forays

It was not until the end of the 1870's that Monet abandoned urban themes in general. Thereafter his modernity was to lie in his technique alone–and in his pro-posed "redefinition" of painting. Before doing so, he worked very extensively on urban and Paris subjects, as did all his friends. In effect, from the mid-1860's the city had been a focus for the artists who later em-braced Impressionism. Well before they went out to explore the rural landscape, they were tirelessly painting scenes of Paris.

a city's shape and form

In 1857, Baudelaire sadly enumerated the changes taking place in "the city's shape". These changes produced the urban landscape of the Impressionists. As young painters they began by describing a relatively

Edouard Manet
View of the Universal Exposition of 1867
(1867).
Oil on canvas:
108 x 196.5 cm.
Nasjonalgalleriet,
Oslo.

Manet chose to paint people amid the diversity and density of buildings, rather than celebrate the grandeur of Napoleon III's régime.
▼

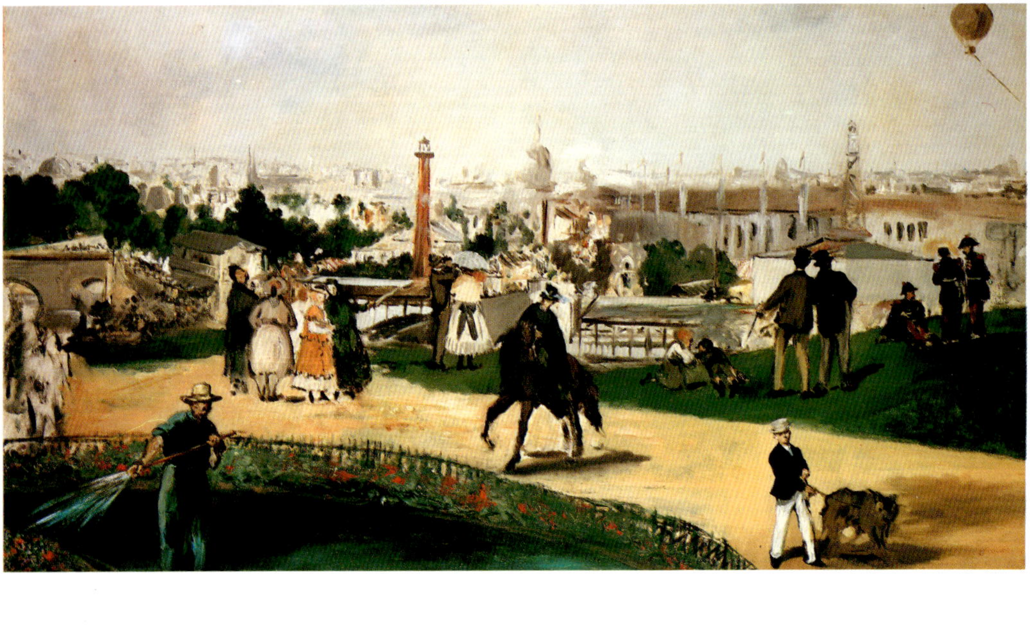

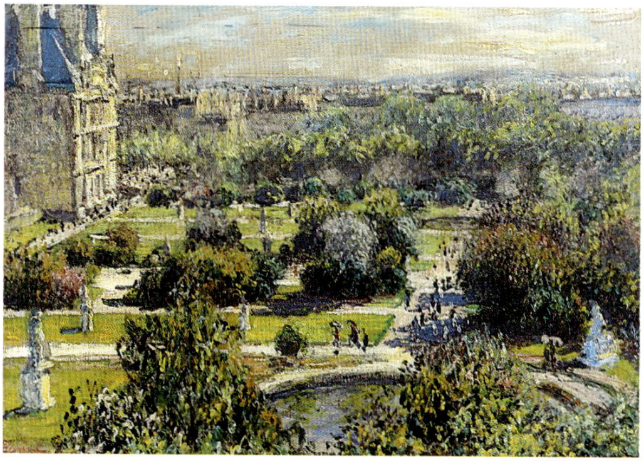

◄ **Claude Monet**
The Tuileries (1876).
Oil on canvas:
54 x 73 cm.
Musée Marmottan,
Paris.

Louvre Museum. By convention, the buildings of the Louvre symbolized past aesthetic glories; but the manner in which these artists gave all the component parts of the urban landscape equal importance constituted a real novelty. What had previously been no more than subject matter for popular engravings and photographs was now appearing in major paintings. In the canvases painted by Monet and Renoir at this time, the passersby, the vegetation and the buildings play an equal rôle and evoke a similar sense of activity.

Paris was then subjected to more ephemeral changes, largely on account of the series of universal expositions which were held there between 1855 and 1900. New monuments suddenly appeared, which the artists only appropriated as subject matter for their paintings, without giving them any more permanence than was their due. Manet, for example, painted the 1867 Exposition, and Seurat the Exposition of 1889.

The Eiffel Tower under construction: 14 July 1888.
Drawing by Fraipont.
Biliothèque Nationale, Paris.
▼

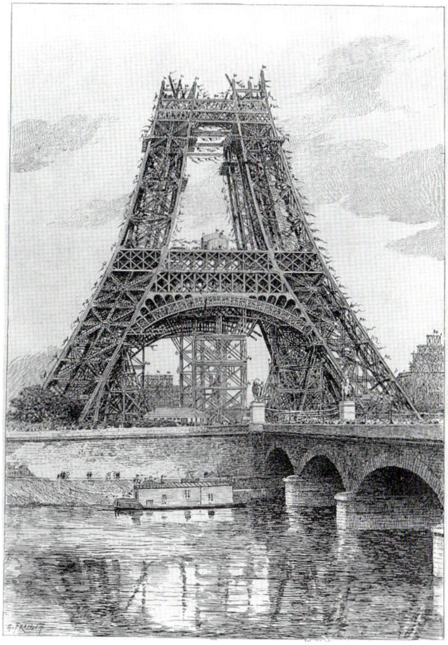

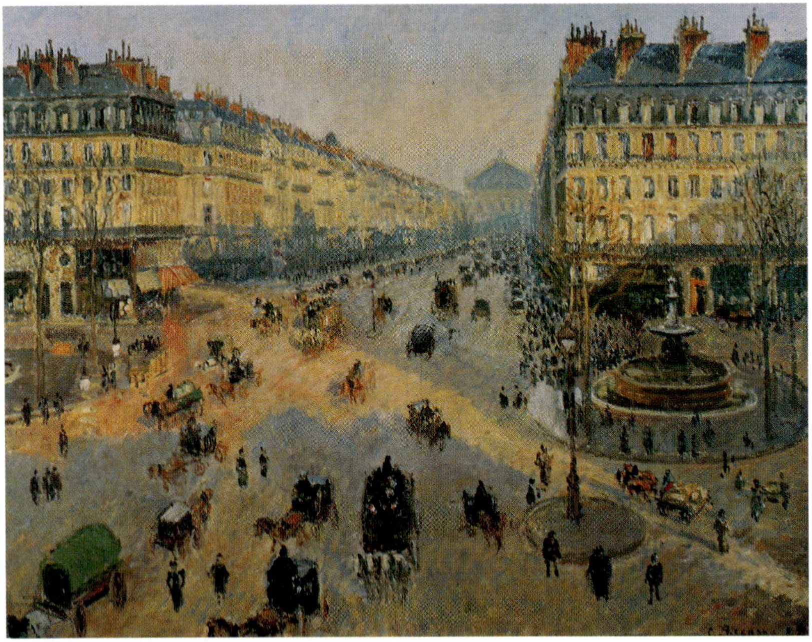

◄ **Camille Pissarro**
Avenue de l'Opéra, sunshine, winter's morning (1898).
Oil on canvas:
73 x 91.8 cm.
Musée des Beaux Arts, Reims.

The stark angles of the architecture and the streets dissolve into the neutral light of a composition traversed by deep diagonals.

citizens and urban views

The 1871 Communard uprising obliterated several major Paris monuments. Only Manet attempted to record this tragic urban event on canvas; for his friends, Paris remained a vibrant, living entity, undamaged by the conflict. Between 1873 and 1877, the Grands Boulevards were the subject of works by Monet, Renoir and Caillebotte, but in the end it was Pissarro who persisted the longest with urban landscapes. He painted Rouen, Dieppe, Le Havre and, above all, Paris, notably the Gare St Lazare quarter, Boulevard Montmartre, Avenue de l'Opéra, the Tuileries and the Seine embankments.

Painting and photography
Pissarro's fidelity to his subject matter can be seen by comparing his canvases with contemporary photographs. But in contrast to the photos, which are framed traditionally, frontally and symmetrically, his approach is always eccentric.

a symphony of the city

The intensity of feeling conveyed to the observer by Pissarro's urban landscapes verges on the symphonic. The artist's approach to his subject was always from above ; in this manner he contrived to impose a general uniformity to its many and diverse characteristics,

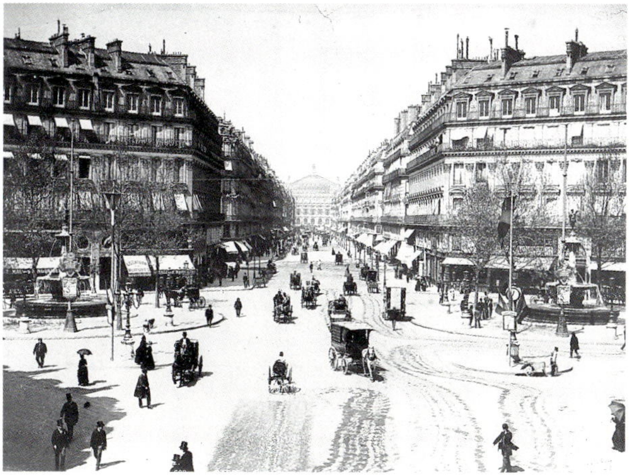

Avenue de l'Opéra. ▶
Photograph
(about 1890).
Biliothèque
Nationale, Paris.

while simultaneously conveying an atmosphere of continual flux. Pedestrians and vehicles are caught in mid-movement, united by a light that appears scattered and diffuse in its overall effect.

Nevertheless, the city as painted by Pissarro is invariably reproduced in its most ordinary guise, though not without grandeur. In the closing years of his life he produced some of the finest cityscapes, in which he set down with admirable truth the peculiar atmosphere and colour and teeming life of the boulevards, streets and bridges of Paris and Rouen.

"I have found a room at the Grand Hotel du Louvre with a wonderful view... I am enchanted at the prospect of doing the streets of Paris which we habitually call ugly, but which are really so silvery, so luminous and so full of life."
C. Pissarro
to his son, 1897.

Camille Pissarro ▶
La Place du Théâtre-Français, Paris (1898).
Oil on canvas:
73 x 92 cm.
County Museum of
Art, Los Angeles.

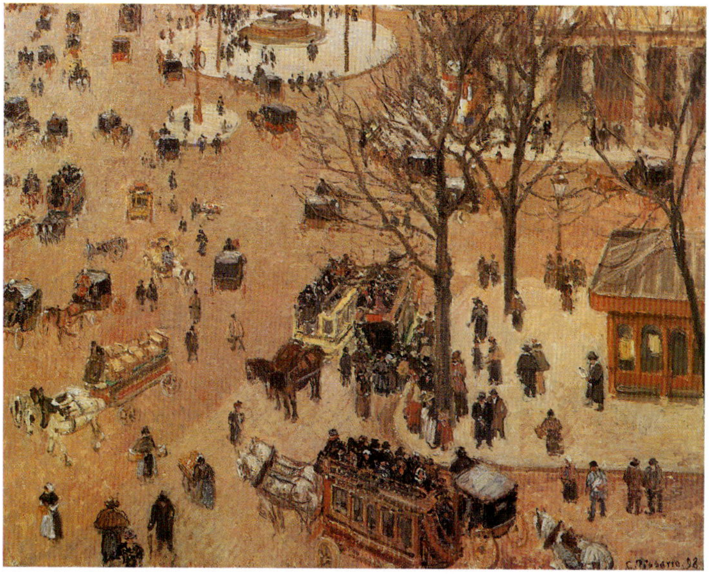

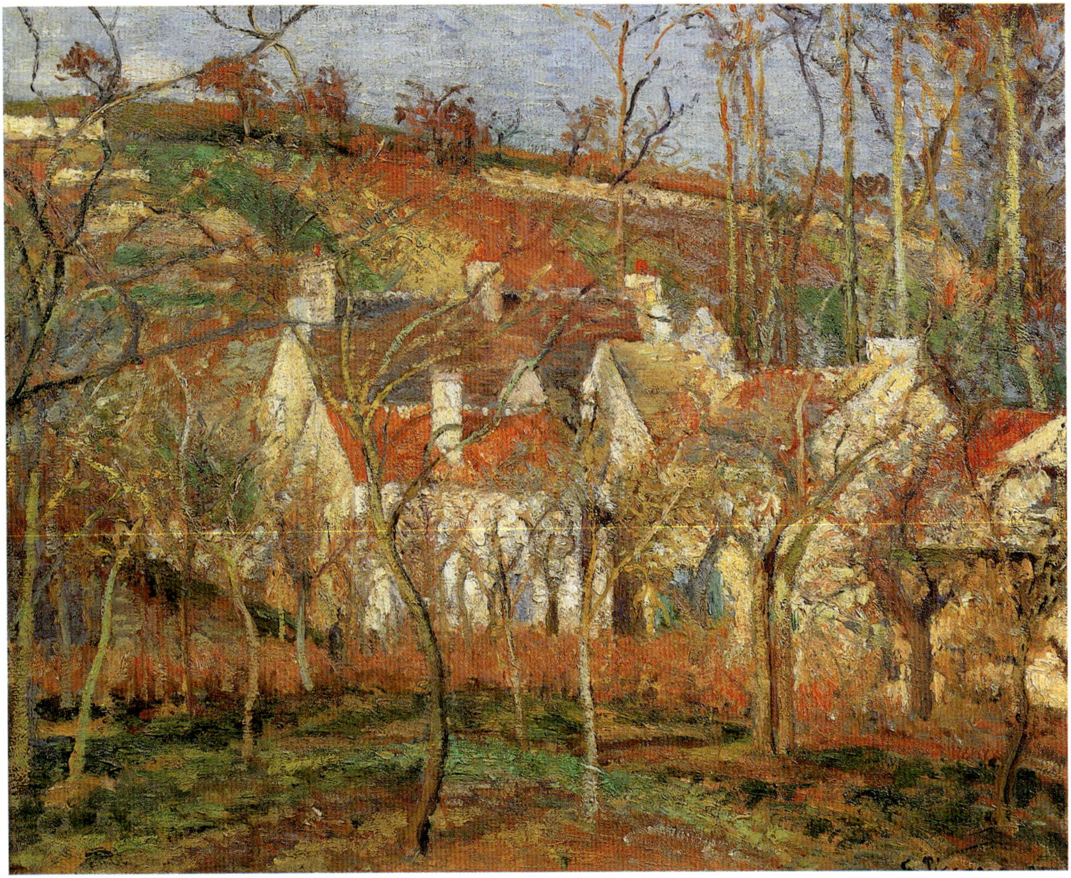

▲

Camille Pissarro
(1830-1903).
Red Roofs, corner of a village, effect of winter
(1877).
Oil on canvas:
54 x 65 cm.
Musée d'Orsay, Paris.

CAMILLE PISSARRO

the reconstruction of nature

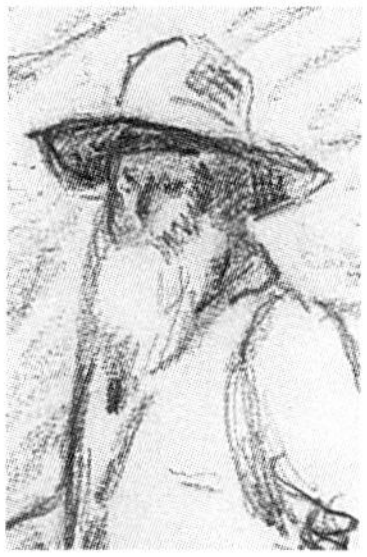

▲
Paul Cézanne
Pissarro going out to paint from life.
Pencil.
Musée du Louvre, Paris.

To paint these few houses at the foot of a hill, a view of striking banality, Pissarro used brief, wide brushstrokes which form a kind of crust. The entire surface has the same density of paint; in its rough unity, this is a real country painting.

Pissarro's subject is not fully readable at first glance. The houses are hidden by a curtain of trees, which closes them into a kind of grid which breaks up the various colour zones. The levels of chromatic intensity are fragmented, shimmering all over the canvas in an explosion of reds interwoven with greens. These colours extend from the central roof to the neighbouring ones, then dissolve into patches of foliage, chimneys, tree-trunks and earth. The same colours, laid on in a similar manner, are featured in both the foreground and the background, in such a way that the unity of the surface is achieved at the expense of its depth. The impasto lends extraordinary solidity to every area of the picture, while the stone buildings, vegetation, sky and atmosphere appear to share exactly the same weight and thickness.

A frequent subject
Pissarro painted several versions of this Pontoise hamlet, a group of houses at the foot of the Côte des Bœufs near his house. Apparently the site caught his interest with its blend of bright greens and blues.

the typical austerity of the land

Pissarro rigorously avoids allowing anything remotely picturesque into this picture, even though the site he was painting is very easily recognizeable as a tiny hamlet in the vicinity of his own home of Pontoise, where the landscape is typically austere.

Rigour and accuracy
Pissarro claimed that he was tired of the "eternal green" of summer landscapes. The bare "effect of winter" he reproduces here offers an accurate image of the French countryside, with no more adornment than the paint itself.

Pissarro and the Pontoise group

Pissarro moved to Pontoise with his large family in 1863, and later returned there constantly, despite his more or less lengthy stays in other places. Many fellow painters came to visit him, staying in and around his village–especially at Auvers–where they formed a thoroughgoing group. Thus Pissarro became the mentor of a whole generation of younger men such as Cézanne, Guillaumin and Gauguin. With them he scoured the surrounding countryside; and separately, or elbow to elbow, they painted their views of Pontoise and the landscape round about.

"Sometimes I dread going back to a picture. I'm afraid I'll find a monster in the place of the precious jewels I thought I had created...yet there are moments of genuine relief, when I discover qualities that are real and solid in myself. Anyway, painting and art in general both enchant me. They're my life–I couldn't care less about the rest."
Pissarro, 1833.

painting straight from life

Physical proximity to the subject was a crucial element of this kind of work, since it allowed the artist to return again and again if he chose. Provided he had the equipment to do so, he could paint in the open air, working directly from life. The goal was to transcribe observations to canvas on the spot, avoiding the filter effect of reorganization within the studio and converting spontaneously into paint that which had been seen in a fleeting moment.
Like all the Impressionists, the members of the Pontoise group were keenly aware of the unity of nature. Occasionally they resorted to a method devised by Monet in the early 1870's, using scores of tiny, light touches and regular crosshatchings to make the canvas vibrate in unison with

Red roofs, corner of a village, effect of winter (detail).
▼

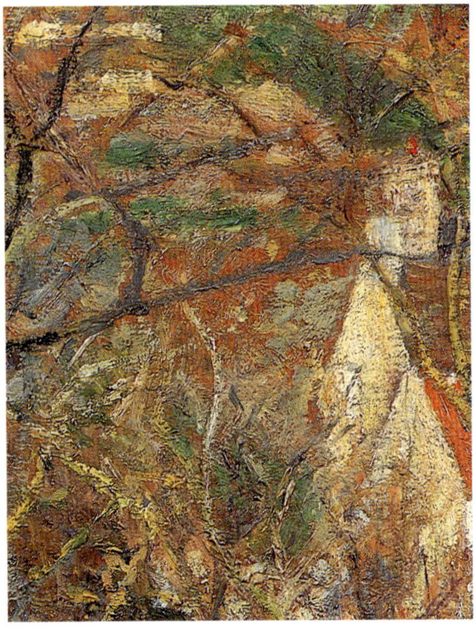

"Cézanne and I were always together, but one thing is certain, we each hung on to the thing that counts, our own 'sensation'. That would be easy to demonstrate."
Pissarro, 1895.

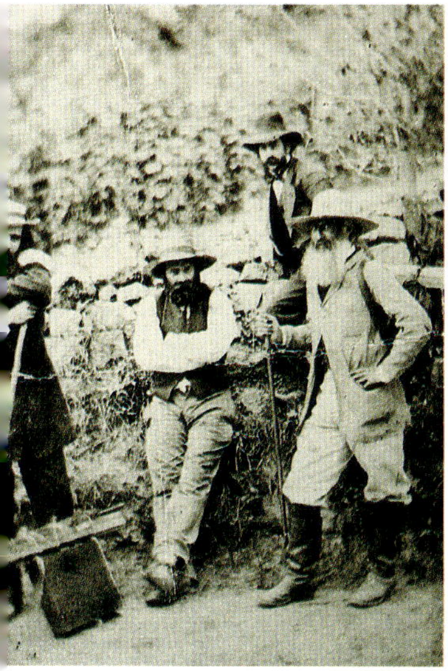

an all-absorbing light. More frequently they sought to impart greater weight to what they felt. Though as time went by they increasingly abandoned their early use of Courbet's palette-knife technique, they did not hesitate to apply their paint as thickly as possible, laying it on in compact, homogeneous layers. In this fashion they contrived to cover the entire surface of the canvas with diminutive "packets" of colour, built up from a succession of abrupt touches. This uniform roughness of surface gave a more constructed character to the representation of nature, without any loss of homogeneity.

◄ *Paul Cézanne* (centre) *and Camille Pissarro* (right) *near Auvers*. Photograph taken in about 1877.

The two men's equipment seems more suited to a mountain excursion than to a painting expedition.

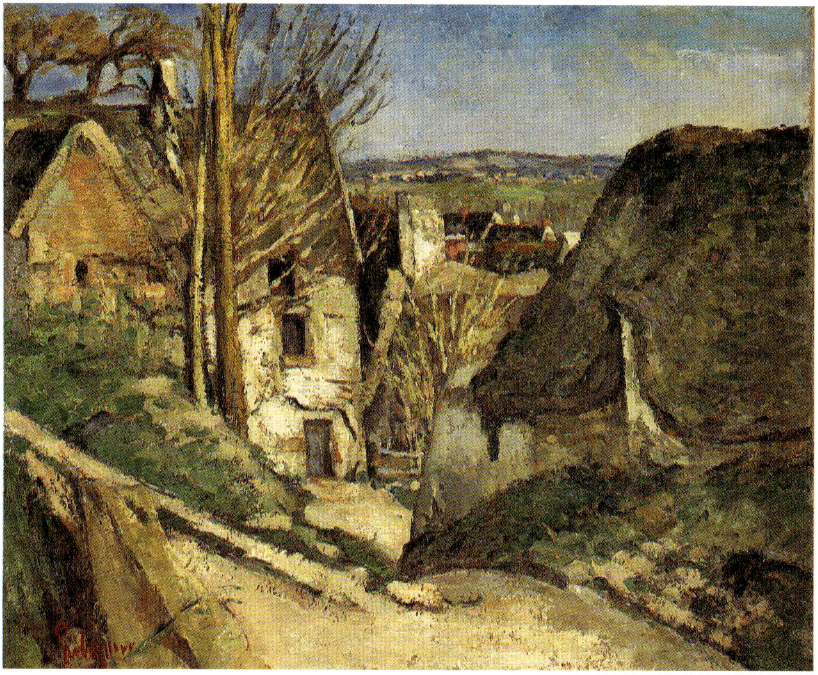

◄ **Paul Cézanne**
The hanged man's house, Auvers-sur-Oise (1874).
Oil on canvas: 55 x 66 cm.
Musée d'Orsay, Paris.

In 1872, Pissarro had Cézanne to stay with him, and shortly afterwards Cézanne moved to Auvers nearby, where he remained for two years.

fixities and fluctuations

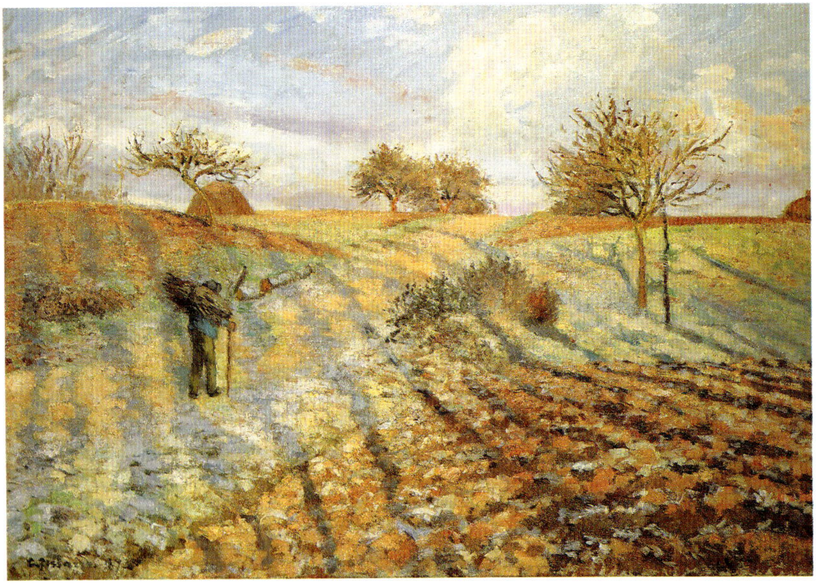

▲
Camille Pissarro
Hoar frost (1873).
Oil on canvas:
65 x 93 cm.
Musée d'Orsay, Paris.

The peasant, an anonymous silhouette, blends into a landscape fashioned as much by the labour of men as by the vagaries of nature.

The degree to which the work of Pissarro and his friends was paradoxical needs to be emphasized. What they did was nothing less than to expose nature as space, demonstrating the simultaneous presence in it of both unstable elements and solidity overall. Mankind, most of the times represented by one or two toiling peasants, is sucked in by this effect of unification. The contrast is perhaps more easily balanced when the light has the effect of darkening the values depicted and blending them into a single mineral corpus. Yet this reconciliation may also be achieved when there is really vivid light in a picture, even though this may require a measure of falsification.

Structuring nature
In his *Hoar frost,* Pissarro structured the space by elongating and simplifying the shadows cast on the ground by a row of poplars behind his back. In this way he can cut across these diagonals with his furrows and lines of frost.

dissolution and construction

The shift from Impressionism to post-Impressionism was eked out in the realm of the landscape, and at its source was the difficulty of holding together the theoretically opposite poles of dissolution and construction. For Monet, Renoir, Manet and even Guillaumin, the

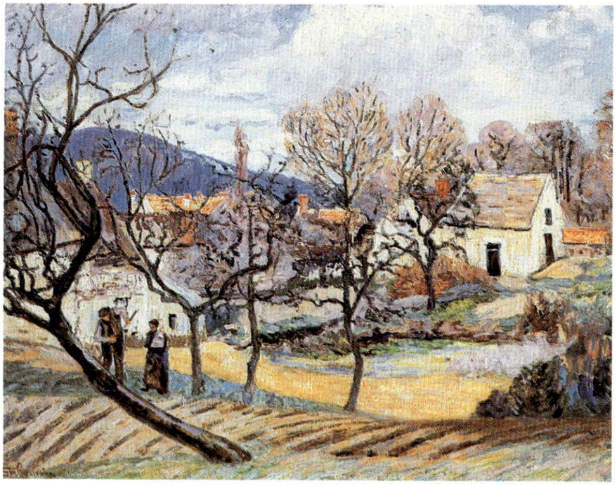

Armand Guillaumin ►
(1841-1927).
Outskirts of Paris
(about 1890).
Oil on canvas:
74 x 93 cm.
Collection
of Mrs Lyndon Baines
Johnson.

solution to the dilemma lay in a progressive dissolution of forms and a lightening of the palette. For Cézanne, the answer was a new kind of construction, which opened the way for a reassessment of the landscape per se. For Pissarro, the quest to reconcile these contradictions continued until the day he died, compelling him to seek new methods, and to experiment in directions which were very difficult to understand, if indeed they were understandable at all. Even so, Pissarro never discovered the all-encompassing solution for which he had so ardently hoped as a young painter in the 1870's.

*"In my view, one should capture nature in the impression of a moment; and preserve that moment forever on canvas, using carefully studied techniques.
Work is the only solid virtue... another step toward truth has been taken, now that artists want their subjects to bask in real sunshine, instead of the false light of the studio."*
E. Zola, 1880.

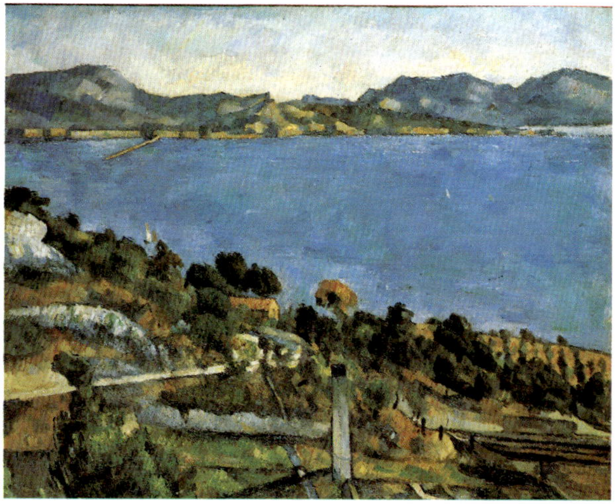

Paul Cézanne ►
L'Estaque; View of the Gulf of Marseille
(1878-1879).
Oil on canvas:
59 x 73 cm.
Musée d'Orsay, Paris.

"It is like a playing card. Red roofs against the blue sea."
Cézanne to Pissarro, 1876.

Paul Cézanne
The red rock
(1895-1899).
Oil on canvas:
91 x 66 cm.
Musée de l'Orangerie,
Paris.

In about 1895, Cézanne's landscapes began losing their readability, as the artist began relying more and more on ordered transverse brushstrokes. Here an orange mass of colour cuts across the view of the forest. The perspective is negated. The rock is more of a flat slash over the surface of the canvas, surrounded by a thick black line, than something that detaches itself, i.e. an object existing in nature.

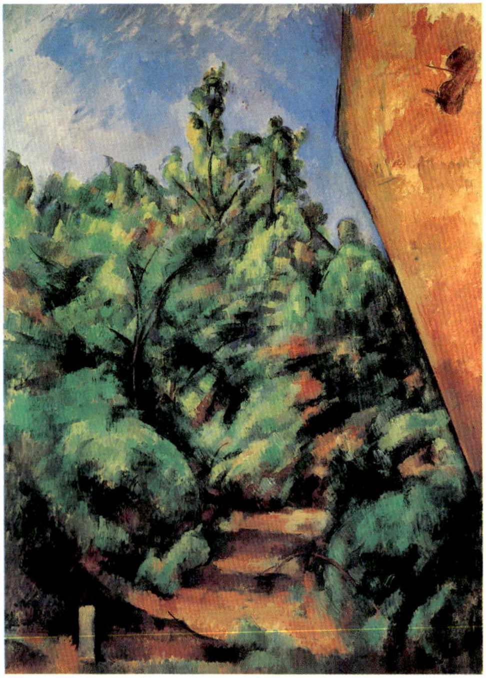

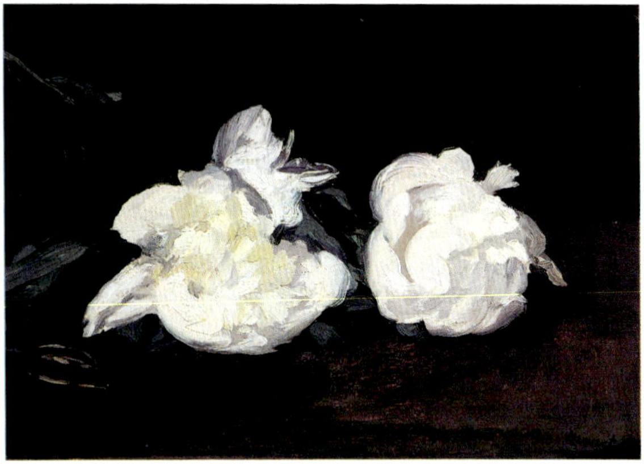

▲

Edouard Manet
White peonies and secateurs (1864?).
Oil on canvas:
61 x 46.5 cm.
Musée d'Orsay, Paris.

At an early stage, Manet's flower bouquets attained a simplicity which rendered the original subject of secondary importance. Here the whiteness of the flower, and the way it is laid out, have become themes in themselves.

Claude Monet
Waterlilies; the clouds
(1916-1923), detail.
Oil on canvas:
197 x 1271 cm.
Musée de l'Orangerie,
Paris.

"The Impressionist sees and reproduces nature such as it is, in other words uniquely in terms of coloured vibrations. He uses no line, no light, no relief, no perspective and no chiascuro, none of those infantile classifications."
J. Laforgue, 1883.

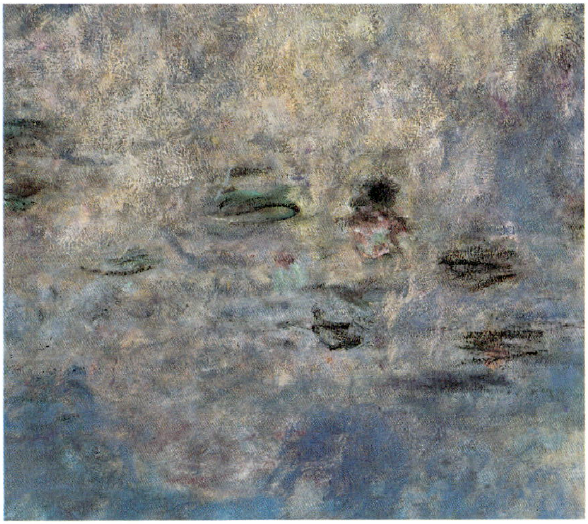

Leaving out the object

The point of departure of Impressionism was a desire to make the most faithful possible rendering, on canvas, of what the artist perceived. This visual fidelity derived from a realist, naturalist aesthetic inherited from Courbet. But for Courbet the most important feature of a given work was its subject matter, which he undertook to reproduce with precision. As far as the Impressionists were concerned, the objects could no longer be given pride of place, given that their goal in painting was not to interpret but merely to represent what they saw. Things were no longer isolated from their contexts, as if they had colours and contours that existed universally. They were always modified either by the light that fell on them, or by the air by which they were surrounded.

The object was therefore treated in exactly the same way as its environment. With every point that might catch the eye receiving equal emphasis, all assumed the same material importance. An area of colour for the Impressionists was no more than an area of colour, no matter what other feature it might be attached to. For them it was no longer possible to make objective distinctions between such areas.

Edgar Degas
At the Dressmakers
(1905-1910).
Pastel on paper:
91 x 75 cm.
Musée d'Orsay,
Paris.

When Degas returned to this theme towards the end of his life, he crushed his pastels so hard against the paper that their spreading colours overwhelmed his realist motif.

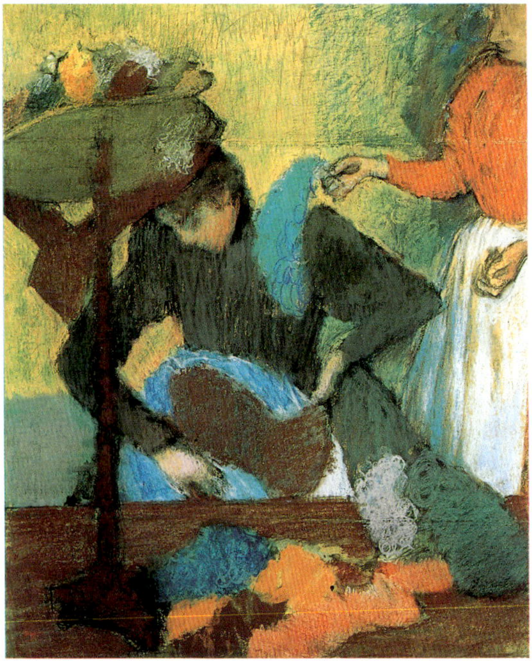

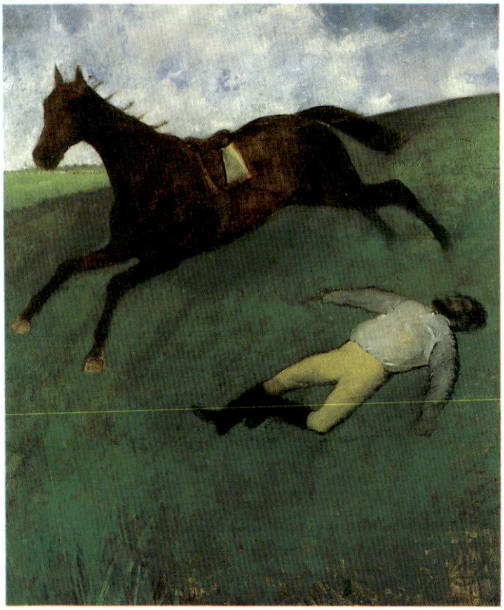

Edgar Degas
Injured jockey
(between 1896-1898).
Oil on canvas:
181 x 151 cm.
Kunstmuseum, Basel.

Paul Cézanne
Bathers
(1900-1906).
Oil on canvas:
172.2 x 196.1 cm.
National Gallery,
London.

Between 1900 and 1906, Cézanne painted three monumental versions of bathers in a landscape, a theme which had interested him since his youth. With this painting his geometrical approach reached its high point.

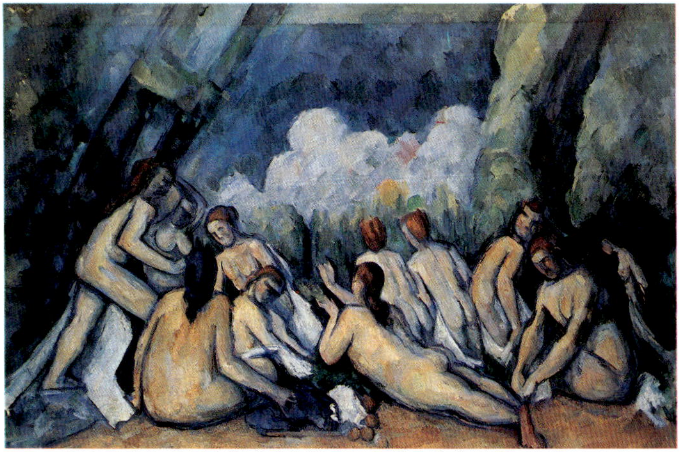

The Impressionist artist followed the logic of his perception, as well as the logic of his painting. By making atmosphere the determining factor in all aspects of nature, he placed everything he painted in the same light, conferring harmony on the ensemble at the expense of material objects.
In his mission to reflect a world which he felt to be fundamentally unstable and elusive, the artist adopted a similarly elusive technique. In order to avoid giving any sort of priority to one feature, to the detriment of others, he abandoned traditional modes of composition. He also used novel points of vantage to break up reality into equivalent fragments of nature. These fragments might extend beyond the frame of his picture–and sometimes made it so foreign to its traditional representation as to be unrecognizable.

With Degas and Cézanne, who stand at opposite extremes of Impressionism, this instability extended to the human figure, which had hitherto remained more or less inviolate. In their work this most important focus of attention because part of the landscape or the décor, without vanishing altogether. Both artists, as they progressed, laid more and more stress on the complex meanings of the objects and figures they painted. Thus when Degas returned to the fallen jockey theme he had first tried in the 1860's, he gave it a deliberately non-naturalist slant, like shadow theatre. In this way the vaguest subjects acquired a paradoxical dimension, vanishing in terms of imitation only to emerge again as re-creation.

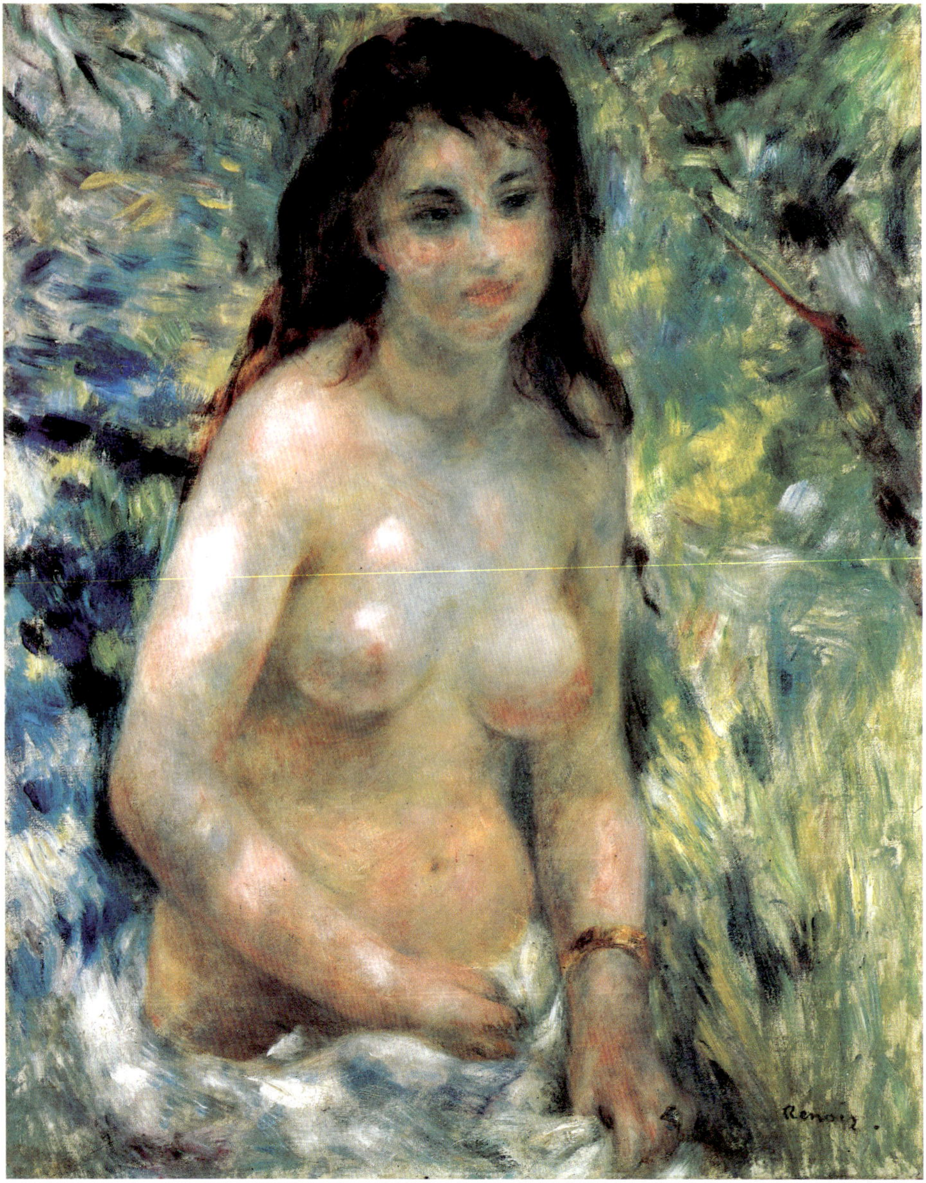
Renoir

AUGUSTE RENOIR

bodies dissolved in light

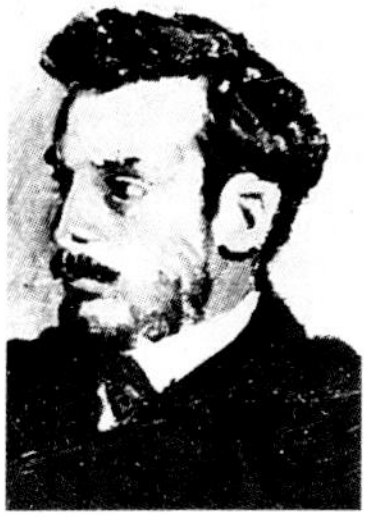

▲ **Frédéric Bazille.** *Portrait of Auguste Renoir* (1887), detail. Oil on canvas: 62.5 x 51 cm. Musée des Beaux Arts, Algiers.

"Someone should explain to Mr Renoir that the torso of a woman is not a pile of decomposing flesh, with the green and violet patches that denote a state of total corpse-like putrefaction." This was the verdict of the Figaro's art critic when this canvas was displayed at the second Impressionist exhibition.

In effect, Renoir had decided to show a work which seemed barely at the sketch stage. The facial features are ill-defined, and the décor is made up of side-by-side brushstrokes which do not cover the bare canvas at the sides and bear only a distant resemblance to vegetation. The body seems to be assailed by the light, which casts small white flecks on the model's torso.

"The sparkle and shade cast by the shifting light...the passing combinations through which reflections create unique or multiple harmonies, are the favourite effects of Renoir." S. Mallarmé, 1876.

the body born of colour

◄ **Pierre-Auguste Renoir** (1841-1919). *Study; torso, effect of sunshine* (1875). Oil on canvas: 81 x 64 cm. Musée d'Orsay, Paris.

The body emerges from a mass of violent, abstract colour, from which it gradually separates itself; the farther one moves away from the face, the less defined is the hair.

Renoir, whose previous contributions to the Salon had met with a certain success, was already established as a skilful technician by the time he painted this. Here he hesitated between fidelity to his subject and pure delight in coloration for its own sake. The model is identifiable as Anna Leboeuf, who died shortly afterwards, and the light effects, which seem at first sight so peculiar, can be attributed to the filtration of sunshine through foliage. All the same the dominant feature is the sensuality of the brushwork in itself, the manner it has of suggesting an undulating caress ("I want to touch", declared the artist), and the way it erases all differences between the human body, the cloth and the vegetation, in the same light-filled harmony.

the nudes of Renoir

The nude was always a favourite subject for Renoir. Yet for many years he forsook his daring exploits of the 1870's, preferring to impart more substance to the female body than to its surroundings. The human body, quite apart from the inhibitions or the appetites it may arouse, possesses a natural plastic quality which is hard to place on the flat surface of a canvas without causing it to stand out. For many years Renoir produced fairly conventional nudes which referred directly to the 18th-century French style or else to a brand of classicism reminiscent of Ingres. But around 1900, suffering from an arthritic condition that made it hard for him to work with a brush, Renoir was induced to call the status of the material object back into question. Everywhere in his later nudes he used the same thick, short brushstrokes, in such a way that the compositions were broadly unified in a kind of softness. All of nature acquired the same sensuality and fullness that he had previously confined to the female body.

Edgar Degas
After the bath
(1896).
Photographic print:
16.5 x 12 cm.
J.Paul Getty Museum,
Malibu.
▼

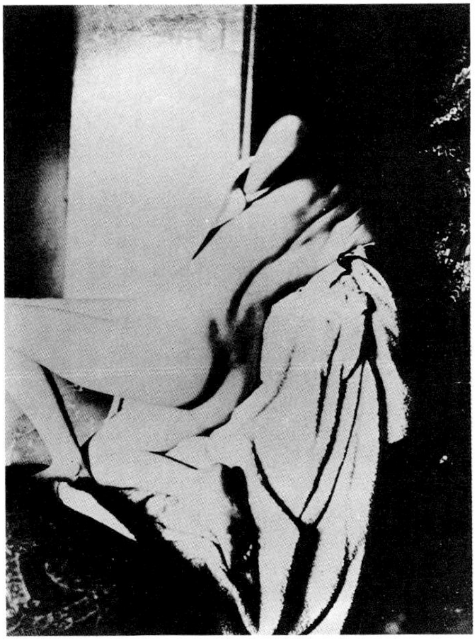

Degas as a photographer
Here Degas' mastery of photography is evident. He used the medium for the same purposes as he used paints and pastels: as a way to affirm the body while submitting it to tensions that break it down.

Degas' voyeurism

His closest friends, such as Monet, tended to avoid nudes, which made it difficult to preserve a painting's homogeneity and detracted from the representation of nature as a unified theme. Only Degas and Cézanne also tackled nudes in any quantity, and each invented his own manner for the purpose. For Degas the use of pastel and monotype

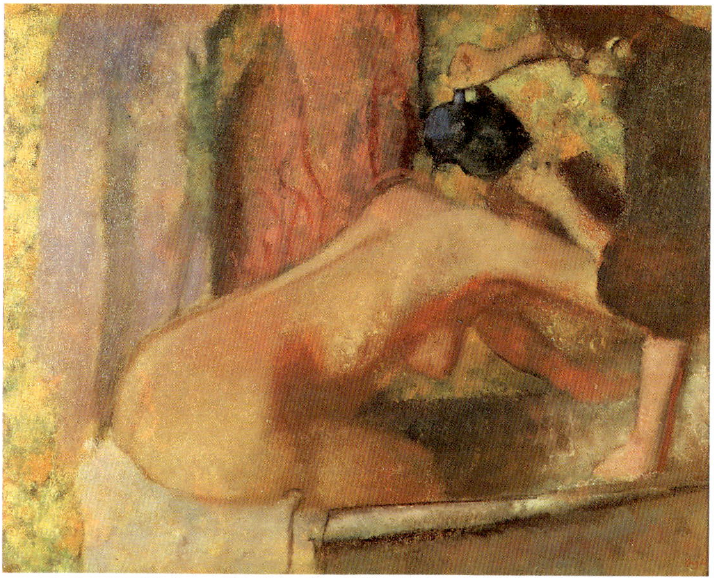

◀ **Edgar Degas**
Woman bathing
(about 1895).
Oil on canvas:
71 x 89 cm.
Fine Arts Museum,
Toronto, Ontario.

In his pastels, photographs and paintings, the nude bathing became a semi-abstract theme for Degas.

served to dissolve his line into colour, which he then went on to pulverize into myriads of flecks. These technical means of neutralizing all emphasis on the human form corresponded to a deepening of the way in which the artist viewed his relationship with the physical reality of others. He acknowledged that he was a voyeur of sorts, enslaved by a desire to see what in physical terms was taboo. As a result, his slant on the human body is fragmentary, scarcely separable from the rest of what he sees. Thus in Degas the body is, so to speak, dissolved by the impulse of the eye.

"The entire subject is physical and sensual, breathing the perfume of life. At this stage, Renoir no longer cared for dryness, and he didn't need realism."
L. Gowing, 1985.

Pierre-Auguste Renoir ▶
Bathers
(1918-1919).
Oil on canvas:
110 x 160 cm.
Musée d'Orsay, Paris.

In 1918 Renoir wrote "I want to mix my landscape with my figures," in compositions "...full to bursting."

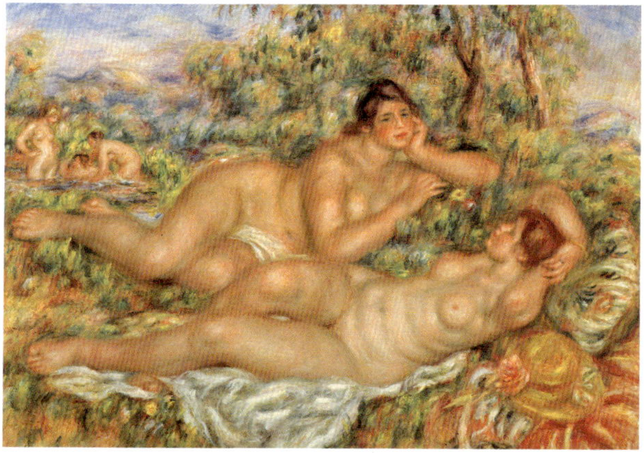

Cézanne's recreation of the human body

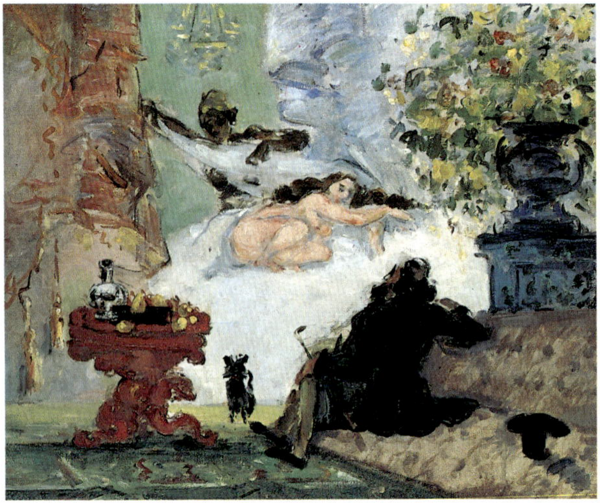

◄ **Paul Cézanne**
A Modern Olympia
(1873-1874).
Oil on canvas:
46 x 55.5 cm.
Musée d'Orsay, Paris.

The artists' Olympia
The scandalous nude which brought about the birth of Impressionism is contemplated by the painter, who sits in the foreground. His desire deforms what it sees and gives it a motion of its own.

In his pre-Impressionist youth Cézanne painted a number of nudes dominated by themes of violence, passion, orgy and rapine. After 1870 he returned to the nude and painted more than two hundred pictures of groups of men or women bathing in the open air. These paintings are frequently hard to understand, given that they seem undecided between insistence on the sculptural nature of the nude and the importance of its fusion with the landscape. The key to them may lie in the two versions of *A Modern Olympia,* which are explicit variations on Manet's painting done in 1869 and 1873.

"Here geometry is also applied as a method of composition: the work is focussed on purely artistic research, with clear leanings toward the abstract. This is why Cézanne has a perfect right to modify the proportions of the human body. The entire outline must tend toward the point of the triangle, as must each part of the body."
W. Kandinsky, 1911.

imaginary bodies

Perhaps out of inhibition, and almost certainly out of necessity, Cézanne never hired a model to pose naked for him. He painted from his imagination, attempting to integrate the bodies he could only dream of into a natural environment that he knew down to its subtlest

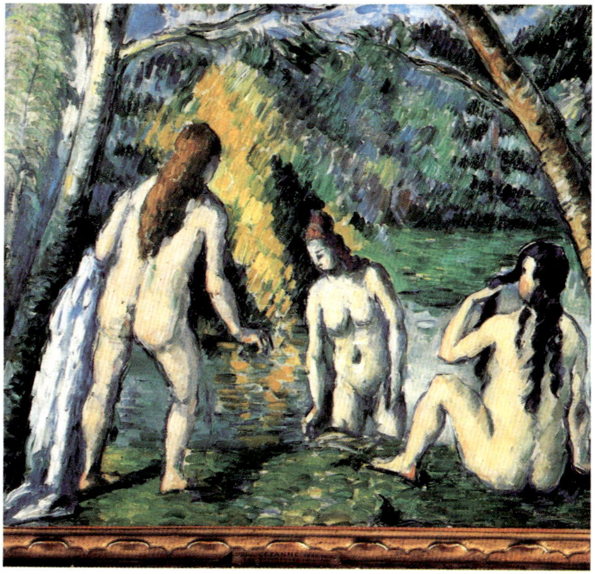

◀ **Paul Cézanne**
Three bathers
(1879-1882).
Oil on canvas:
53 x 55 cm.
Musée du Petit Palais,
Paris.

This work once belonged to Matisse, who claimed that it had given him "moral support at critical moments."

variation of light. The paint handling was to be the same throughout the composition. It became more and more regular as the theme developed, culminating in small areas of light which opened on to one another. Nothing in either the coloration or the brushwork distinguishes the bodies from the landscape, which is entirely innocent of relief. Everything obeys the dual logic of the eye and of the transcription of nature to the canvas: a "parallel to nature", as Cézanne called it. The real objects have no existence independent of their environment and the light that bathes them; in the painting they are all reconstructed in the same way, which emphasizes their geometrical aspect without reference to their obvious form. Thus the human body is no longer a basic given, but evolves from the painting. And in the painting it loses itself.

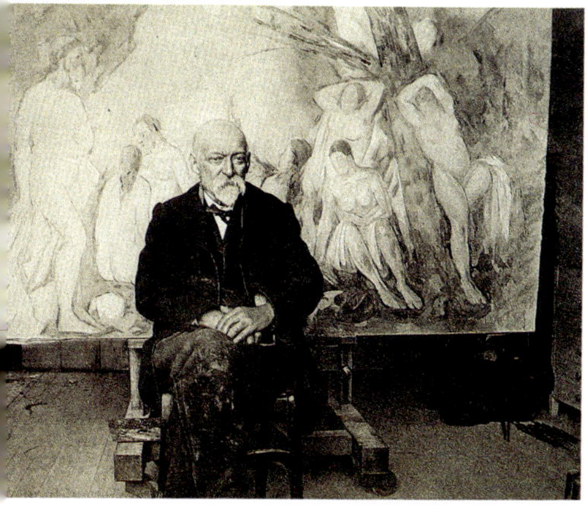

◀ *Cézanne and his 'Bathers'*
(painting now at the Museum of Philadelphia).
Photograph by Emile Bernard, taken in March 1904.

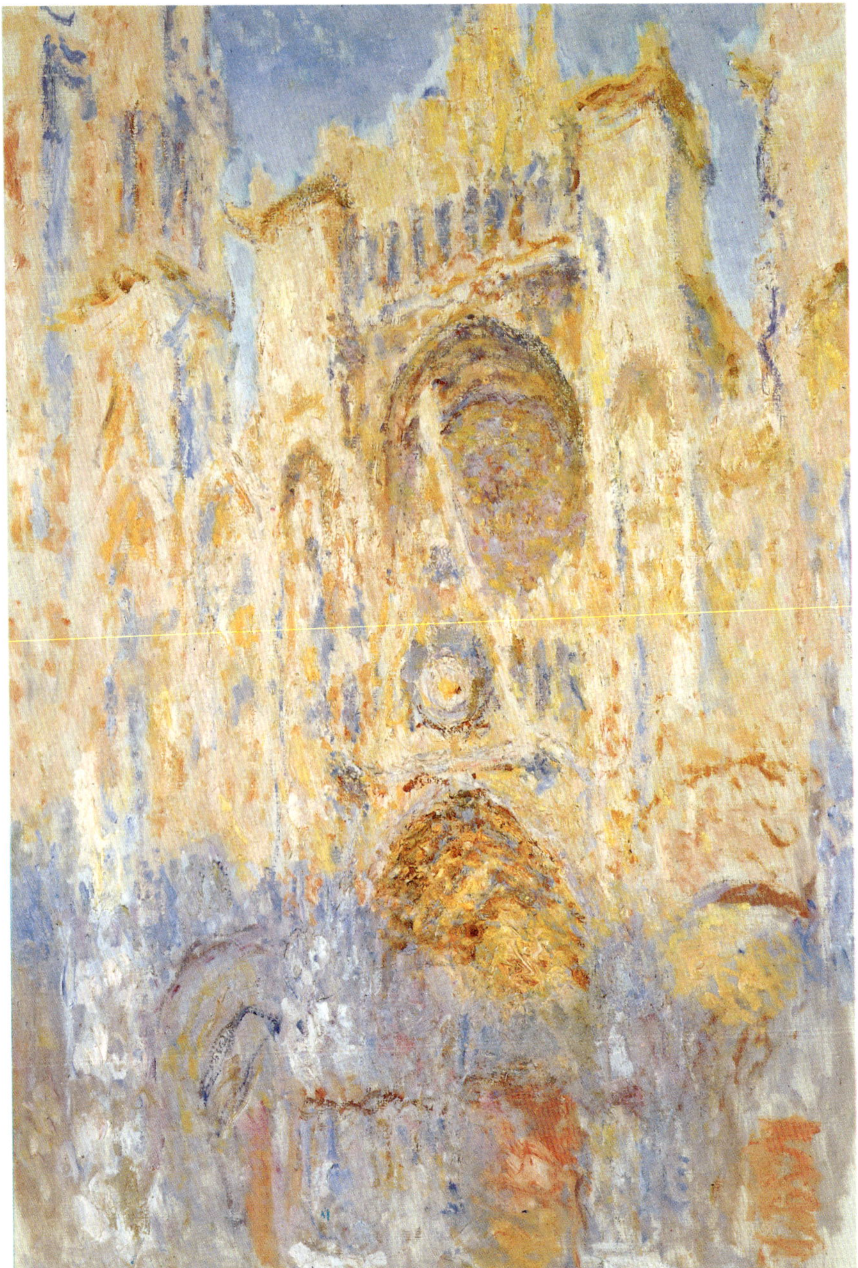

CLAUDE MONET

the discovery of series painting

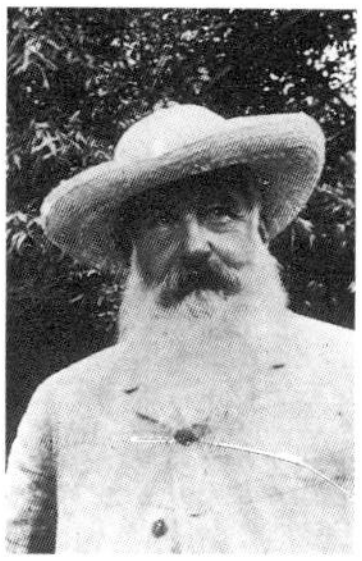

▲ *Claude Monet in his garden at Giverny* (about 1915), detail. Photograph by Sacha Guitry.

A first look at this painting reveals little more than an impression of shimmering points of colour. And then, because of the outline of the sky, you begin to discern the portal of a Gothic church. The subject has lost much of its significance; at this stage it is no more than a pretext for an uncontrolled explosion of colour.

Paradoxically, it is the masonry, the hardest, most constructed element in the picture, which is most dissolved by the light. The artist achieves this result by adopting a point of vantage so close to his object that the façade of the cathedral and the surface of his canvas are virtually united on a single plane. Only the great blue zone of the sky and the slightly oblique perspective introduce any kind of division. The bright colours are laid on in thick masses, which do not blend into the outline of the architecture and even tend to make it unreadable.

The breakdown of line
The porches of the cathedral crumble into a multitude of mauve, blue and orange tones; it is hard to say what differentiates them, without reference to the cathedral itself.

the liberation of colour

Naturally, as a good Impressionist, Monet began with a study of his subject at different times of the day and the year. The distribution of the colours was first of all a response to close observation of the light received by the building in the evening, which has the effect of flattening its reliefs and suffusing its shadow zones with reddish iridescence. But in reproducing "...what lay between the subject and myself" he abandoned the subject altogether. His colours were now justified by the requirements of the painting as an entity.

◄ **Claude Monet** (1840-1926). *Rouen Cathedral. Effect of sunlight. End of the day* (1892). Oil on canvas: 100 x 65 cm. Musée Marmottan, Paris.

Monet: the instant visualized

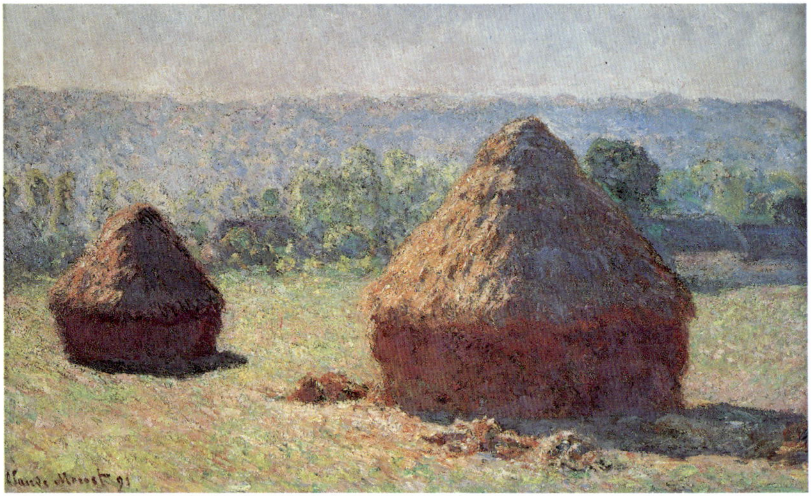

▲
Claude Monet
Haystacks, late summer, morning effect
(1891).
Oil on canvas:
60 x 100 cm.
Musée d'Orsay, Paris.

In 1891, the Durand-Ruel Gallery in Paris exhibited 15 canvases on this subject, the first real series in the history of art.

Monet painted over thirty versions of Rouen cathedral from a similar angle. Of these he exhibited about a score side by side at the Durand-Ruel Gallery in 1895, as he had done four years previously with his fifteen Haystacks. At that time he made it clear that "these works only have value by comparison with, and as part of, the complete series". Thus Monet initiated a serial mode of painting, in which what changed was not the object (this remained identical), but the manner used to paint it, in the most material sense of the term. Only the colour and the treatment altered.

Jean-François Millet
(1814-1875).
Autumn: Haystacks
(1869).
Oil on canvas.
Metropolitan Museum of Art, New York.
▼

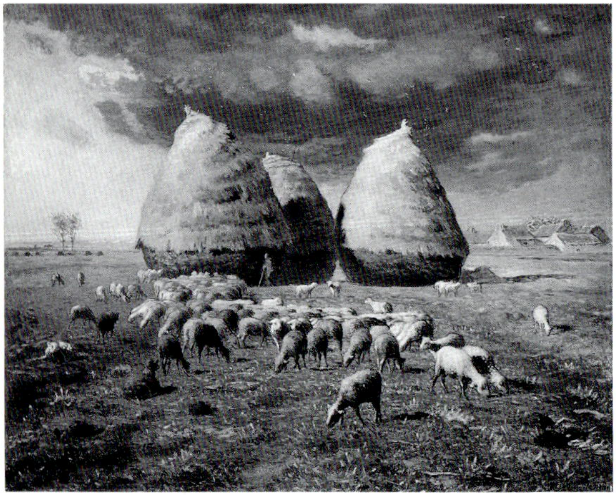

the culmination of impressionism

The invention of the series epitomized the desire of Impressionists to bring their movement to its logical conclusion. The aim was to give value to the most fleeting instant. And what better way to do this than to show how every moment

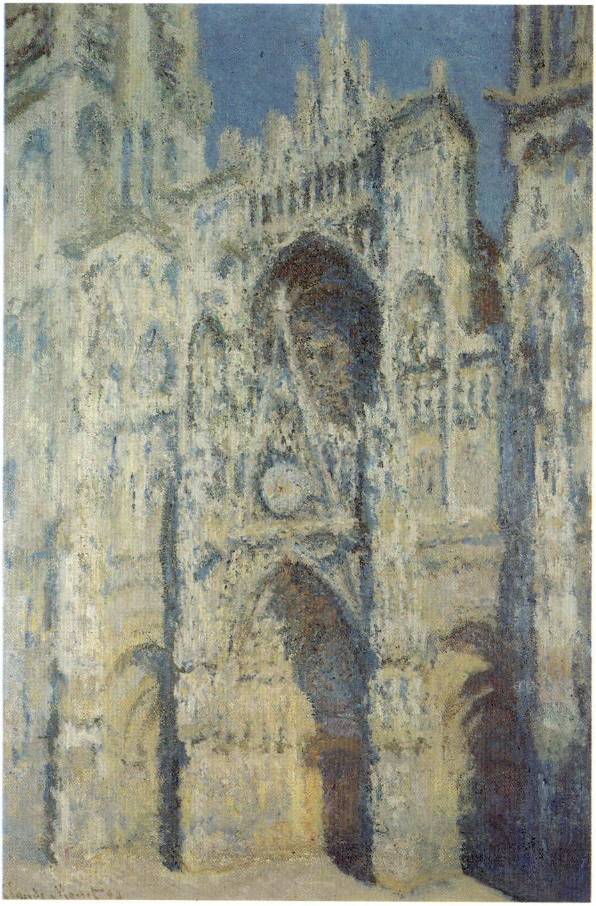

◄ **Claude Monet**
Rouen Cathedral: harmony in blue and gold, full sunshine (1891-1894).
Oil on canvas: 107 x 73 cm.
Musée d'Orsay, Paris.

The series
The idea of handling the same motif in several variations was adopted by many artists in the 20th century. The series offered abstract painters an opportunity to concentrate on certain clearly-postulated problems, and to use the rigorous methods of scientific research.

has its own separate interest, even when nothing but the weather has changed? As to the rendering of atmosphere, this is done by neglecting the objects it contains. Naturally, this quest for instantaneousness in painting, for materialization of the immaterial, is impossible to carry out, for the painting of a picture takes a certain amount of time and demands specific materials. Monet eventually abandoned his open-air dogma and took the paintings in his series back to his studio, where he carefully and comprehensively reworked them. Spontaneity came through in the apparent disorder of his brushwork, and intangibility in the thickness of his paint.

Monet's series
When Monet began painting series in the 1890's, he concentrated on the pictural qualitites of the work, at the expense of the object matter. When he painted his haystacks or poplars, he avoided reference to rural themes. When he painted his cathedrals, he made no statement about religion. As he stated in 1895: "The subject is unimportant in itself."

the picture and the object

All the Impressionists' still lives reflect a similar paradox. The objects in them seem empty of substance; they are little more than pigment and binding material mixed against a piece of fabric. This is what Manet's flowers and fruits so superbly declare, the more so because they are rendered in isolation: the fibres become brushstrokes and the shadows are transformed into patches of colour. *Asparagus* is probably among the most significant of these works in terms of the story behind it. More important than the anecdote was Manet's demonstration that from henceforth painting would be less inspired by nature as by an earlier painting.

A splendid gesture
In gratitude to Charles Ephrussi, who paid 1000 francs for *A bunch of asparagus*, though it was priced at only 800, Manet sent him this painting with a note saying: "There was one missing from the bunch."

the impressionist paradox

"The object and the subject are irremediably in motion, elusive and un-arresting. To achieve the flash of identity between the subject and object, is the mark of genius."
J. Laforgue, 1883.

A paradox lies at the heart of Impressionism, even though it only emerged in the light of day when the group began breaking up following the 1880's. In their desire to represent objects in the true light of their

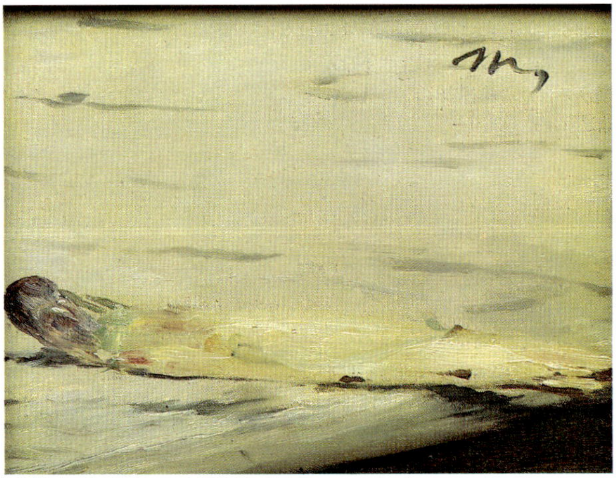

◀ **Edouard Manet**
The Asparagus (1880).
Oil on canvas:
16 x 21 cm.
Musée d'Orsay, Paris.

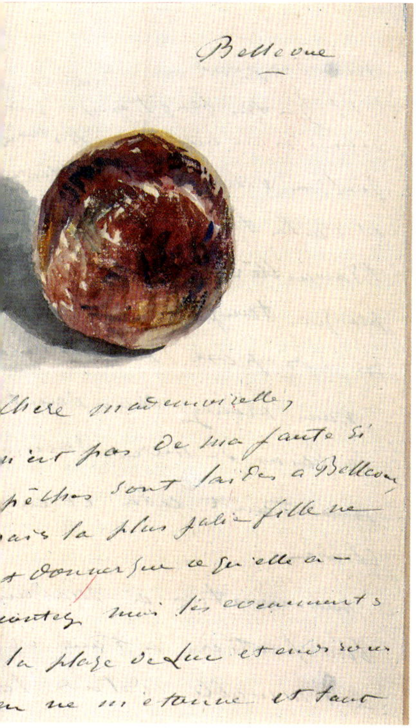

natural existence, the Impressionists were led to neglect them in favour of the air and light which surrounded and penetrated them. By attempting to paint only what they saw–everything they saw–they ended up laying most emphasis on their means of making it visible. Ultimately, the painting must obey the logic of perception as much as that of pictural creation. For every one of the Impressionists, these considerations quickly created a conflict, which each of them dealt with as well as he could. Monet, after the experience of his series, chose to create a garden at Giverny whose elements were meant to be painted rather than lived. In this way he remained loyal to his visual sensations, given that these were preplanned to be "pictural". Nature itself could thus be made to obey the painter's logic...

◄ **Edouard Manet**
Mirabelle Plum (1880).
watercolour on a letter to Isabelle Lemonnier: 20 x 12.5 cm.
Musée du Louvre, Paris.

Claude Monet
Morning, weeping willows
(1916-1926).
Oil on canvas.
Triptych, each panel 200 x 425 cm.
Musée de l'Orangerie, Paris.
▼

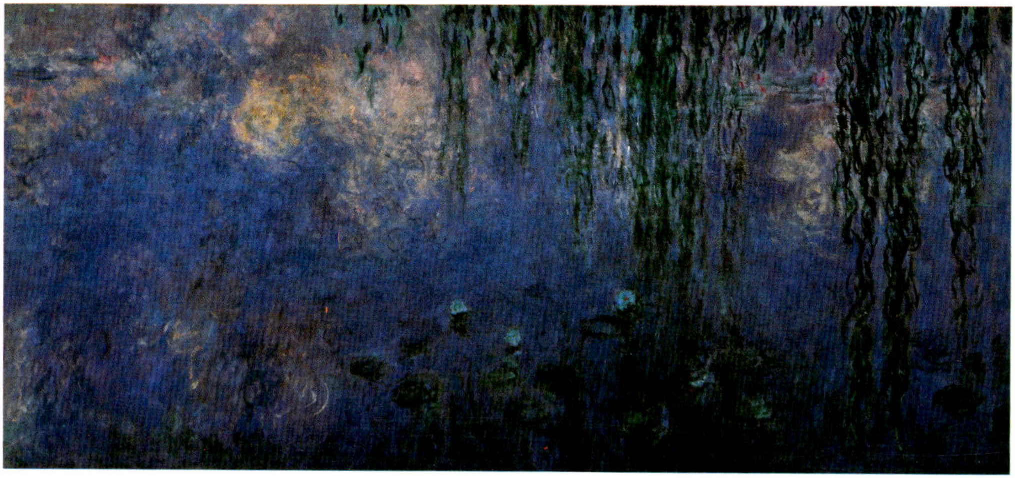

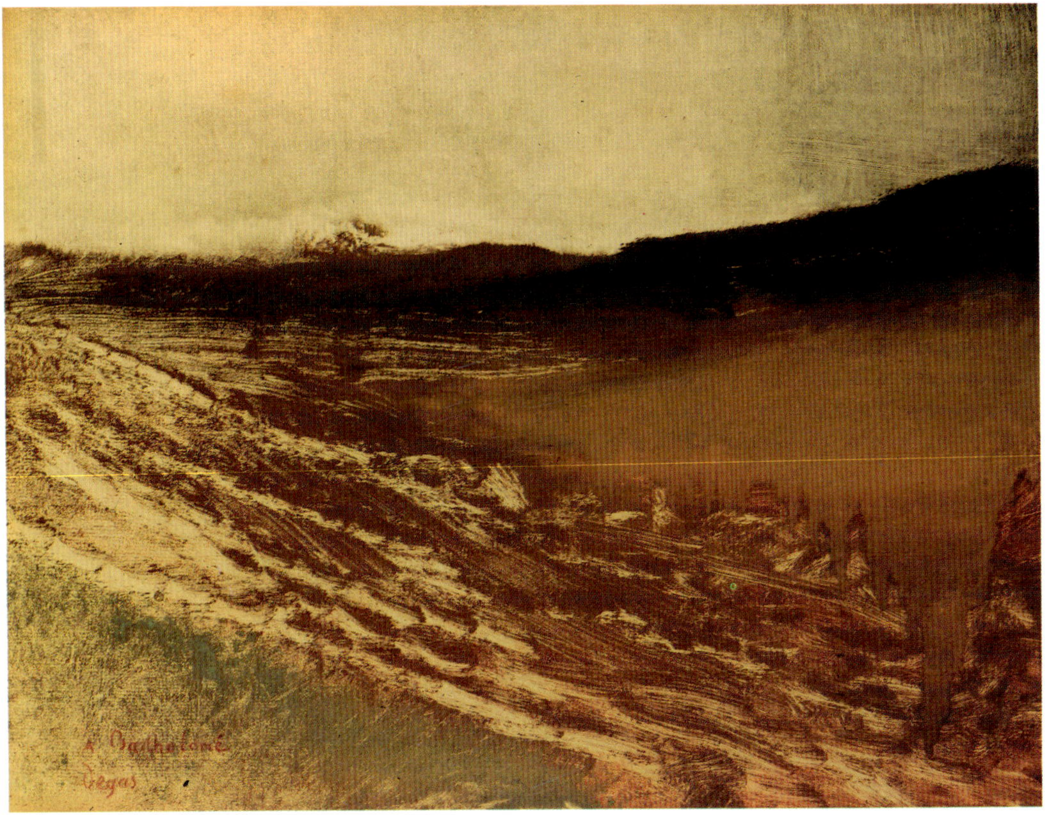

▲

Edgar Degas
(1834-1917).
Landscape, also called
Landscape in Burgundy
(1890-1892).
Colour monotype
on cream paper:
30 x 40 cm.
Musée d'Orsay, Paris.

EDGAR DEGAS

the work and the process

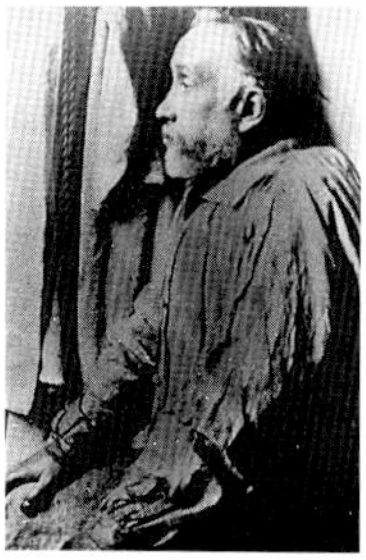

▲
Degas in his studio (about 1898). Photograph attributed to Bartholomé. Bibliothèque Nationale, Paris.

The title of this painting tells us it's a lanscape without specifying which one exactly. Nonetheless it is hard to see in it anything other than a juxtaposition of patches of drab colour, which in places seem to have dripped randomly.

Degas often showed hostility to those of his fellow Impressionists who were dogmatic about open-air painting. He even said he would be happy to empower the police "...to shoot those wretched men lurking in the greenery, on their stupid white canvas stools". When he painted landscapes, he did it altogether differently. In October 1890, he travelled to Burgundy: 2-1/2 years later, he announced that he had printed 21 monotypes of the trip, mostly from his memory of riding in trains and coaches, with no specific localities mentioned. Degas claimed that these monotypes represented "states of the the eyes" rather than "states of mind".

The monotype
Monotype was Degas' preferred technique in the matter of prints; it involved painting on a zinc or copper plate, and then printing the result on paper. Monoprints are usually unique, because the succeeding printings become paler and paler. Degas often touched up his monotypes with pastels.

painting as a process

One might add that in this case the print represents a "state of manipulation". The landscape emerges from the manner in which the artist lays on his colours. Several elements, such as the sky, are evoked purely by the white of the paper. The thin black layer of the clouds is striped with hatchings. The red furrows are defined with sweeping brushstrokes, or perhaps with the painter's fingers. The brown patch against the earth is a way of showing that the art here is based solely on Degas' use of the painting process.

Degas' manifold tech-niques

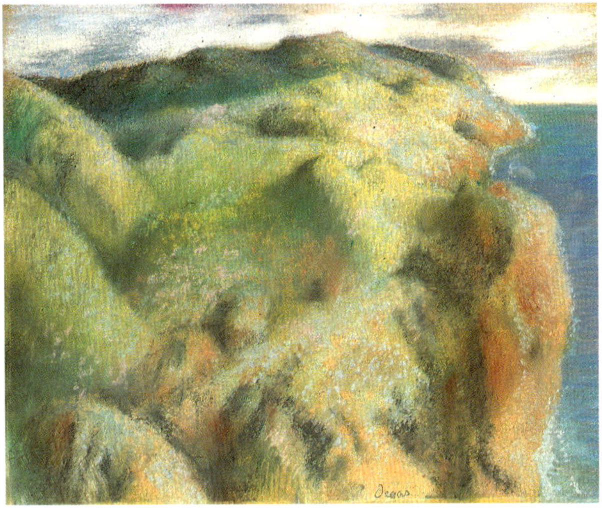

◄ **Edgar Degas**
Landscape (about 1892).
Pastel on monotype: 42 x 55 cm.
Jan Krugier Gallery, Geneva.

This work metamorphoses a landscape into a nude.

After the 1880's, Degas continued to lay emphasis on the processes involved in his work. He tried every technique. Often he painted on unprepared canvas, which absorbed colours and left the grain of the fabric behind. At other times he used very dry pigments which formed a fine powder on the surface, or else blends of oil and pastel. The print was the area of choice for these manipulations, which invariably detracted from the importance of the original subject matter. The pictural effects were much more important. The reality referred to could only exist in the

"It is singularly difficult, in these landscapes, to penetrate the secrets of M. Degas' trituration of matter... this is all one wants to do... at times it is as if he were a child making mud pies."
A. Alexandre, 1892.

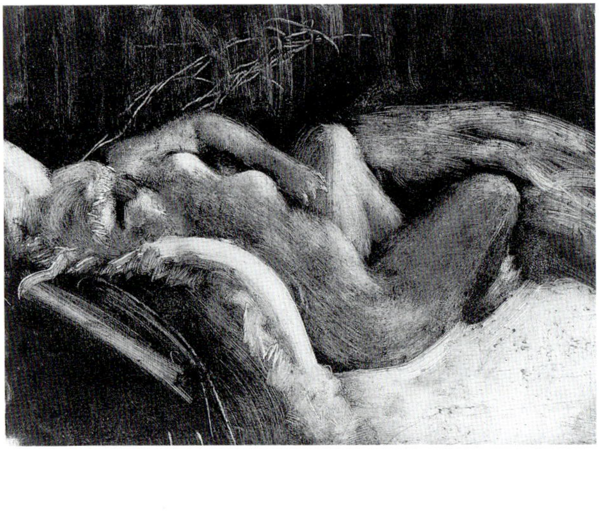

◄ **Edgar Degas**
Reclining nude, also called *Sleep* (about 1879-1885).
Monotype in black ink on cream-coloured paper:
27.6 x 37.8 cm.
British Museum, London.

context of its materialization, in other words in the procedure whereby it existed in terms of art. By the same token, a monotype of a nude could be changed into a landscape by the addition of pastel, and the sense of a scene could be entirely modified by alterations to its original state.

To each his own type
All the Impressionists tended, as the years went by, to view a certain type of figuration as a generic pattern, transmissible to all other subjects. Degas and Renoir opted for the nude, Monet for green landscapes, and Pissarro for urban views.

the painting as a new form of nature

These metamorphoses reached their culminating point with Degas, but nearly all the Impressionists found themselves involved with them in the later stages of their lives. It was as if they had discovered, by wrestling constantly with the same motifs, that the way they were rendered was the most important thing of all. With Monet, who had fought to preserve a strong sense of naturalism in his work, old age accentuated the importance of the pictural process. Nearly blind, he went on painting, using very thick brushwork. His pictures were constructed in a riot of encrusted colour. Monet no longer reproduced nature. He was nature.

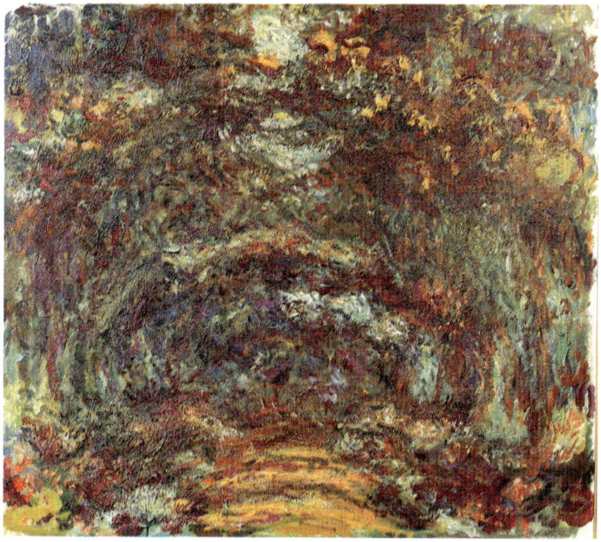

◄ **Claude Monet**
The rose-alley at Giverny (1920-1922).
Oil on canvas: 89 x 100 cm.
Musée Marmottan, Paris.

Cézanne: brush-work as a basis

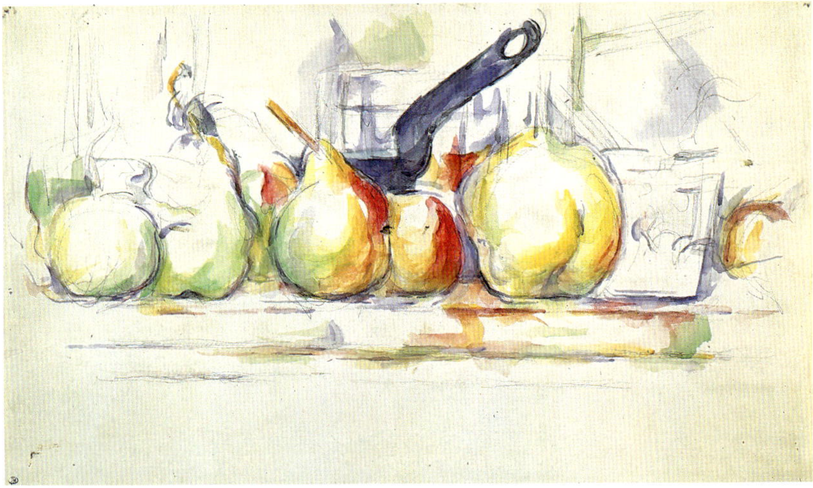

▲ **Paul Cézanne**
Apples and pears
(1900-1904).
Watercolour and graphite pencil:
28.1 x 47.8 cm.
Musée d'Orsay, Paris.

Instead of imitating what was before his eyes, Cézanne laid on his colours in a regular progression–from red to yellow, yellow to green, green to blue.

"There is no tone, and no relief–only contrasts. These contrasts do not spring from black and white, but from a colour sensation."
Cézanne.

Cézanne pursued the idea of the work as an autonomous process much farther than anyone else. He had always been interested in the constructed aspect of his paintings, to the point that they never really answered the criteria of those for whom art should imitate reality. His involvement with Impressionism enabled Cézanne to understand that it was possible to unite logical construction with true representation of nature. In the 1880's, when he was living at Aix, he began to work much more systematically. He gave up his criss-cross brushwork, which tended to impart a confused, vibrant feel to the surface, in favour of a directional manner, meaning that each part of the work was composed of juxtaposed touches of similar thickness, length and direction.

precursor of cubism

It may be concluded that the task Cézanne set himself was not to render what he saw, but how he saw it. For example, he used small rectangular dabs to represent the successive points of impact of his eye. A still-life, a mountain, a building, all have the same value from this standpoint. There is no more form to them: everything is one, and each element opens into the others. The

From Impressionism to Cubism
With his insistence on the geometrical, unified and logical aspect of painting, Cézanne blazed the trail for the artists of the next century, notably Braque and Picasso, whose desire to invent a new realism was called Cubist.

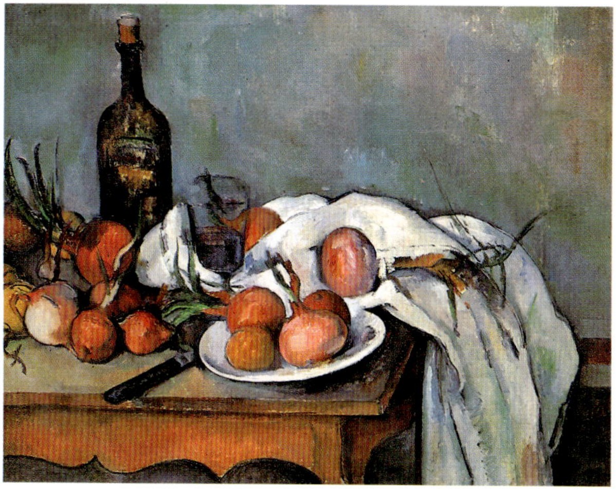

◄ **Paul Cézanne**
Still-life with onions
(1895-1900).
Oil on canvas:
66 x 81 cm.
Musée d'Orsay, Paris.

For Cézanne, every object had its point of furthest extension toward the light, and he worked from this point, arranging his brushwork concentrically around it.

result is a universal, eternal ideal of nature, of which objects are only ephemeral and characteristic aspects. But Cézanne went even further. For him, the painting had to establish a "harmony in parallel with nature". In his 1890-1900 watercolours, he applied this principal fully and for the first time. The forms were painted with one or two patches of colour, whose placement obeyed a logical progression. In the paintings that followed, the entire surface was structured in this way, evoking a geometry which Cubism was later to exploit. The object melted entirely into the structure of the painting.

Paul Cézanne
Black castle
(1904-1906).
Oil on canvas:
74 x 94 cm.
Musée Picasso, Paris. ►

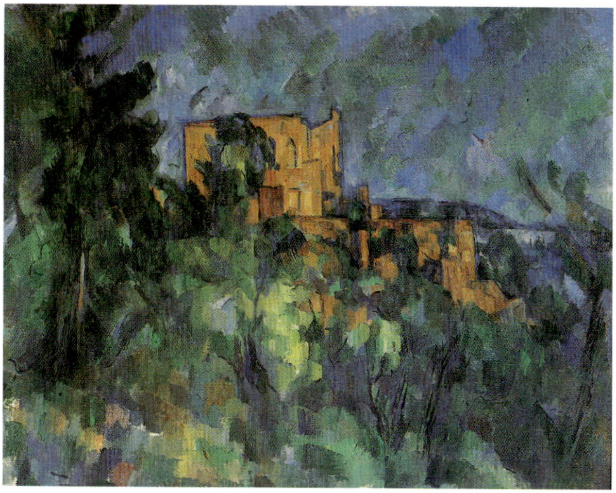

"I immediately understood that his work was guided by a rule of harmony, and that all these modulations had a pre-ordained direction in his reasoning. His perspective was located more in his brain than in his eye."
E. Bernard, 1907.

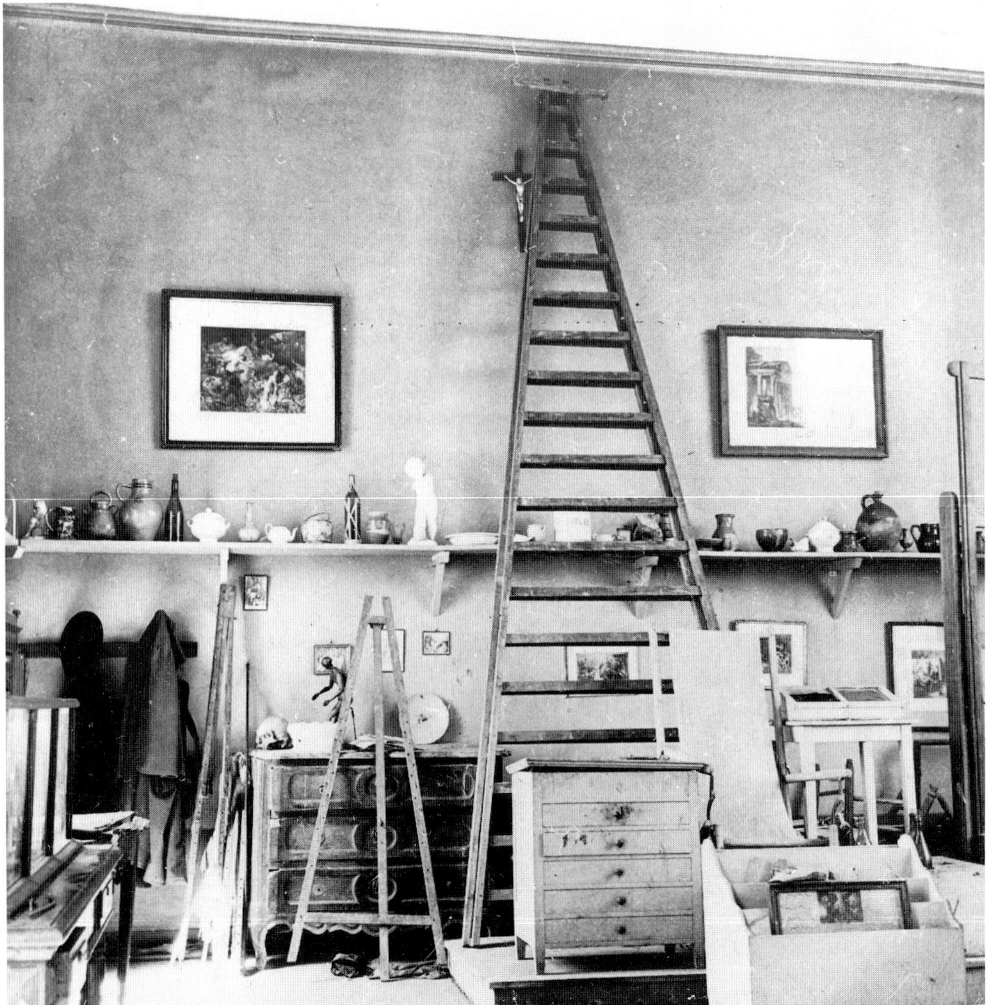

▲

Cézanne's studio at Aix.
Photograph.

A step-by-step analysis

PAUL CEZANNE

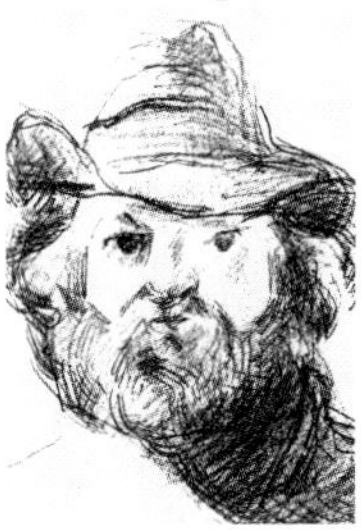

▲
Camille Pissarro
Paul Cézanne
(1874).
Drawing.
Musée du Louvre,
Paris.

Cézanne belonged to the Impressionist group in the early days and adopted its precepts in 1873, even though he altered them to suit himself afterwards. A close friend of Pissarro, he frequented the Café Guerbois and his paintings were shown at the first Impressionist exhibition at Nadar's in 1874.
Nevertheless he retained his marginal status, which eventually branded him a heretic. Despite his family's wealth, he affected rough manners, exaggerated his Provençal accent, and dressed like a peasant. Once he appeared at the Café Guerbois and shook everybody's hand but Manet's, remarking: "I'll not shake your hand now, M. Manet: I haven't washed in a week". This, apparently, was his own peculiar way of expressing his deepest admiration.

a crude approach to impressionism

«<To look> is, and at the same time is not <to eat> and <to be eaten>. (Cézanne? every object reflects the next.) Which means that a continuity exists, whatever its nature, between the observer, the space and the objects.»
J. Johns, American painter, 1977.

The crudity of Cézanne's paintings reflected his nature, and it was years before the critics began to see rigorous principle in them, rather than crass clumsiness, Cézanne's principle being: "I owe you the truth in my painting".
Cézanne was an Impressionist apart, since his work contained the seeds of a new generation in art, but he was an Impressionist nonetheless. After his withdrawal to Aix-en-Provence in the 1880's, he dedicated his efforts to painting what he saw before his eyes: the landscape around the Montagne Sainte-Victoire, objects at his house or in his studio at Les Lauves, prints and copies of works by artists he admired, skulls, furniture, and above all apples and pears scattered about.

In this painting, the **subject** is reduced to almost nothing: a dish containing two biscuits and a few apples, on the lid of a chest, only the upper part of which is visible. Clearly Cézanne started out with something he had before his eyes. The most ordinary reality was enough to start him painting. The objects in the picture are completely prosaic; they probably represent the frugal meal of a peasant in the vicinity of Aix-en-Provence. So this is a theme from real life, **a modern theme**.

The painter used bright colours. Positioned against a neutral brown background, the still-life is disposed between a band of cold tones (blue-green) and warm ones (the ochre of the chest). There is a lateral distribution of **chromatic qualities**: the pale blue and the pink of the biscuits on the plate echo the different reds and ochres of the apples. Your first impression is that Cézanne has used a limited palette for this painting. But if you look more closely, you see that there are many **nuances** of colour in it. Every apple is a cluster of small zones of yellows, reds and whites, rather than a single red which is more or less dark according to the degree of luminosity. This makes it possible to render all the subtleties of the Mediterranean sunshine on the objects, without too much recourse to the variation of chromatic values, in the style of the academic painters.

In this still-life, there are two incongruities: these are the two tree-branches with one or two leaves placed symmetrically on the top and bottom of the composition. Their placement **begs the question**: are they ornamental or real? The blue-green may be wall-paper, but it spills over the chest in several places. If what we see below is really a small branch–the artist seems to have wished to give it a certain volume–then how does it stay up? In truth, we cannot possibly know what, precisely, it is.
Every constituent part of the picture has the **same unstable material and spatial status**. Some of the apples look like flat discs, just like the plate itself, which seems to tilt forward. The empty spaces between the things are handled with just as much care as the rest–one could almost touch them. It is as if the air and the light had acquired solidity, because they seem to act on the objects they surround, and are themselves transformed in return. One can no longer quite tell objects and background apart. They no longer have separate existences.

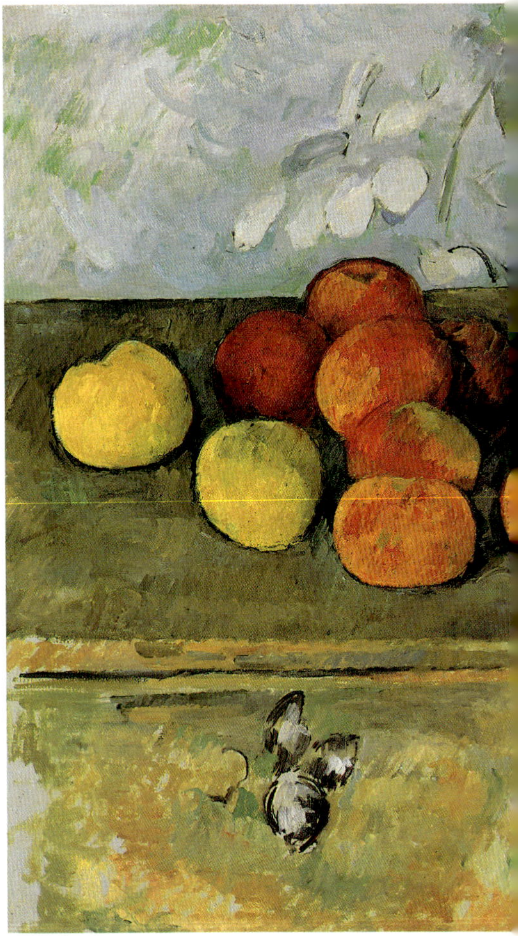

▲
Paul Cézanne
Apples and biscuits
(1879-1882).
Oil on canvas:
46 x 55 cm.
Musée de l'Orangerie,
Paris.

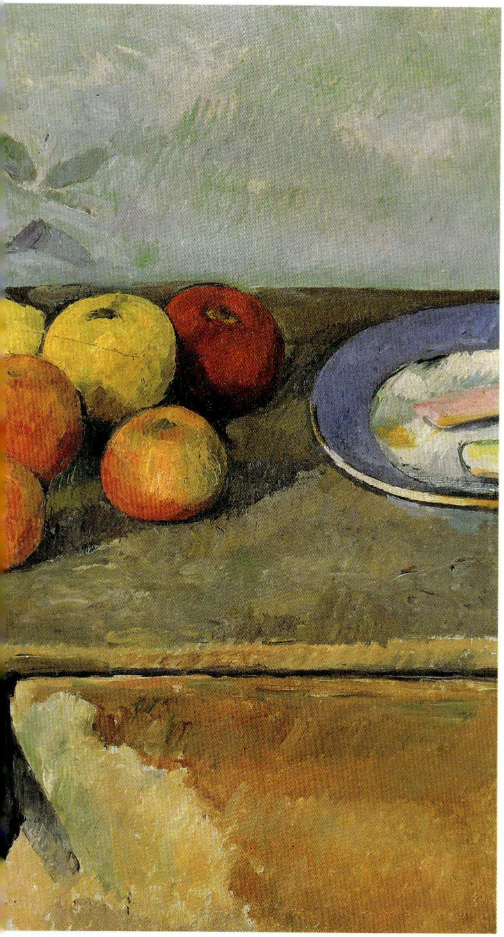

This indistinctness between forms and background also derives from the way Cézanne has structured his **composition**. This is framed in a way that appears indiscriminate. The plate and the biscuits are abruptly cut off on the right hand side of the canvas. The division of the surface into three parallel horizontal bands increases the impression of randomness, in which no element is more important than the others. What we observe is a piece of nature, which could be extended outwards on every side.

Cézanne has covered his canvas with small rectilinear **brushstrokes**, which he has not attempted to conceal. The composition plays a subsidiary role, since it neither contains nor curtails the objects. It merely emphasizes them. What gives them a certain coherence is the regularity of the brushstrokes on the right-hand three-quarters of the picture, where they are nearly all diagonal. In the left-hand zone, by contrast, the work looks more agitated, less regular, and there is even a patch of **bare canvas**. Prior to the early 19th century, this unfinished quality was strictly confined to painters' sketches . Here it is used for a picture of wholly different intent; for with Cézanne one cannot rightly distinguish between a finished and an abandoned painting.

Thus the real emphasis here is on the **pictural process** itself, by which the artist creates the painting. The objects are no more than a pretext, one element among others. For Cézanne, more perhaps than for any other Impressionist, the real subject of a picture was not just a still life. It could also be rich in tactile, erotic, gustatory and symbolic associations–in *Apples and Biscuits*, Adam and Eve, or even the Judgement of Paris, spring to mind. The still life as such is on an equal basis with all the other plastic elements the painter has used in its representation.

Things are only comprehensible in the context of their environment, and the artist is obliged to communicate the fundamental instability of the world: even when, like Cézanne did, he seeks to give it a certain solidity. Things may only be seen by way of their inscription on canvas, and thus the painter is forced to endow the means at his disposal with an importance they never had before.

Biographical notes

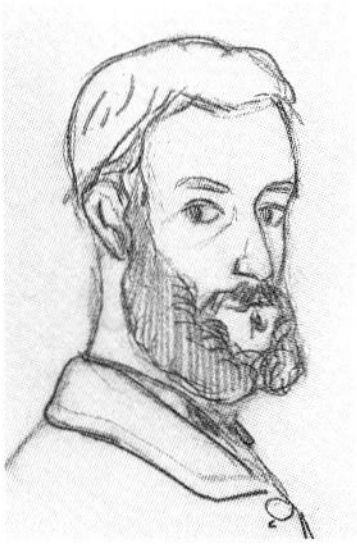

Frédéric Bazille

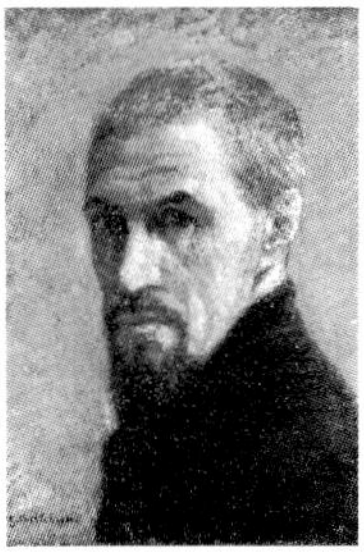

Gustave Caillebotte

■ French painter, born into a wealthy Montpelliérain family in 1841. Bazille was early attracted by art; he was notably inspired by the collection of Alfred Bruyas, a friend of Delacroix and Courbet.

■ 1862, his parents allowed him to move to Paris, where he divided his time between his medical studies and painting. He made friends with Monet and the other future Impressionists while studying under Gleyre.

■ A generous figure, Bazille shared his studio and his meals with less fortunate friends like Monet and Renoir, and bought their paintings. He also worked with them in the Fontainebleau forest (1863), and at Honfleur (1864) and Marlotte (1865-66).

■ Nearly every summer he went back to the Montpellier region to visit his parents. Here he painted his most beautiful paintings, which were portraits done in the sunlit countryside.

■ On France's declaration of war with Prussia, Bazille joined a regiment of Zouaves. He was killed on November 28, 1870 at the battle of Beaune-la-Rolande.

■ Because he died so young, Bazille had no time to develop the significant life's work which his early paintings–*Family Reunion* (1867), *View of a Village* (1869) and *Bathers in Summer* (1870)–seemed to promise. A meticulous, even laborious worker, he was extraordinarily modest. Though he was convinced of the need for open air work, he adhered to the end to a classical manner inspired by Courbet.

■ French painter, born in Paris, 1848.

■ For many years, Caillebotte was no more than an amateur painter. But because of his friendship with Monet and Renoir, he became one of the first collectors of the Impressionists, thanks to the fortune he inherited at his father's death in 1874.

■ In 1876 he took part in the group's second exhibition, and joined Pissarro as one of its prime movers. Thereafter he found himself constantly trying to patch up ruptures and disputes between the Impressionist.

■ After 1885 he painted less and less, preferring to devote his time to his garden and to making sailboats.

■ Caillebotte died at Gennevilliers in 1894. By a will written in 1877, he donated his entire collection to the state, on condition that it be hung at the Louvre. Because of the reluctance of the administration and of the academic painters to accept this bequest, only a part of his collection of Impressionist paintings will be acquired by the Musée du Luxembourg.

■ Caillebotte's rôle as a patron and devoted friend to others overshadowed his own work. Based on careful construction and numerous preliminary studies, his paintings often seem arid; their subject matter, is frequently urbanism in itself. Caillebotte favoured curious angles, and liked painting scenes from high overhead (*Boulevard seen from above*, 1880); he also portrayed figures from behind (*Young man at his window*, 1876), and foreshortened his perspectives (*The Pont de l'Europe*, 1877). At the end of his life, his handling became more free and his paintings less cluttered, with astonishingly sharp colours (*Fruit on a stand*, 1882).

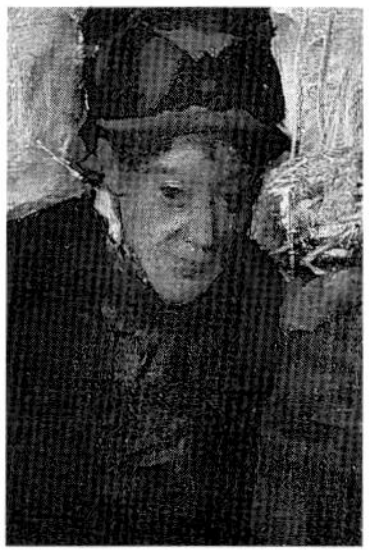

Mary Cassatt

■ American painter, born Pittsburgh, Pennsylvania, 1844.

■ From 1861-1864, Cassatt studied at the Fine Arts Academy, Philadelphia. Prior to 1873 she travelled all over Europe, with Paris as her base.

■ In 1874, Degas noticed Cassatt's *Portrait of Mme Cartier* at the Official Salon, where her paintings had been shown as of 1868. The two became close friends.

■ After 1879, Mary Cassatt took part in all the Impressionist Exhibitions, except that of 1882 which she boycotted out of solidarity with Degas, who had been banned by Caillebotte. Her first exhibition in the US, in 1895, was a failure.

■ Cassatt bought a number of her friends' pictures, and took advantage of her social position to show and sell pictures by innovative painters, for example by organizing tea parties at her apartment on the Rue Marignan. In 1874 she began advising her friend Louise Havemeyer, recommending that she purchase important Impressionist paintings.

■ 1894, Mary Cassatt bought the Château de Beaufresne at Mesnil in the Oise valley, where she spent most of the following years. With the onset of blindness in 1914 she ceased to paint, and she died at Beaufresne in 1926.

■ Mary Cassatt's work, which is relatively little known in France, is highly valued in the USA. Her manner and her subject matter are similar to Degas' (*At the Opéra*, 1878). Like Degas, she was a master of printing techniques, notably dry-point, aquatint and pastel. After 1880 her main themes were mothers and children.

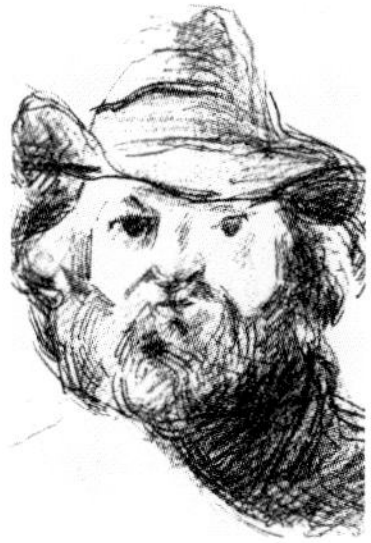

Paul Cézanne

■ French painter, born at Aix-en-Provence in 1839.

■ The son of an Aix banker, at 22 Cézanne obtained his family's permission to embark on a career as a painter in Paris. There he joined a childhood friend, Emile Zola, and attended the Académie Suisse, where he met Pissarro. He also became an habitué of the Café Guerbois, where his coarse manners were a byword.

■ Cézanne was consistently rejected by the salon until 1882. His *Portrait of Achille Emperaire* caused a scandal when it was submitted to the 1870 jury, which suspected him of mocking the official institutions by showing an ugly dwarf.

■ In 1873, Cézanne lived for a while with Pissarro, after his father refused to receive his mistress, Hortense, and their son. He took part in the first Impressionist Exhibition, at which his paintings baffled not only the public but also Degas and Monet.

■ In the last thirty years of his life, Cézanne lived in the Aix region and painted dozens of different views of the Mont Sainte-Victoire. In 1886 he was used by Zola as the model for the mad painter in his novel *L'Oeuvre*, an episode which put an end to the two men's friendship. A marginal figure even among his contemporaries, he became the hero of the new generation just before his death in 1906.

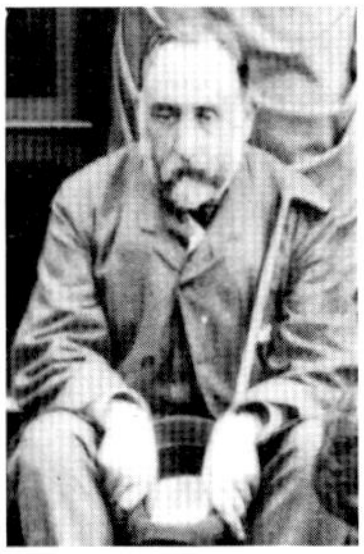

Edgar Degas

■ French painter, engraver, sculptor and photographer, born in Paris in 1834.
■ Degas belonged to a banking family; in 1854 he began taking art lessons with a student of Ingres, the master he was to venerate all his life. He spent much of his time copying at the Louvre, travelled to Italy, and regularly exhibited paintings at the Salon until 1870.
■ As a friend of Manet's, Degas participated in the organization of the 1874 Impressionist exhibition. His ambition was to be the "classic painter of modern life"; he rejected open-air painting and advocated the new brand of realism which eventually prevailed at the fifth and sixth Impressionist exhibitions. But his intransigeance made him more and more isolated, and he broke definitively with his former friends over the Dreyfus affair, when he showed such a violent anti-Semitic streak that he refused to speak to associates like Pissarro and Halévy merely because they were Jews.
■ Alone and blind by 1910, Degas died in Paris in 1917, in an apartment filled with beautiful works by Ingres, Delacroix, Cézanne and Gaugin.
■ With his solid academic background, Degas quickly excelled at portraiture (*the Bellelli Family*, 1867). He painted the places and gestures that typified modern urban existence: racecourses, cafés, concert halls, women at work. He also painted from daring angles and adopted a highly personal approach to perspective (*Absinthe*, 1876). In 1880 he began using ballerinas and nudes at their toilet as virtually his only subject matter, employing every possible technique (oils, pastels, sculpture, monotype) in a period of intense experimentation.

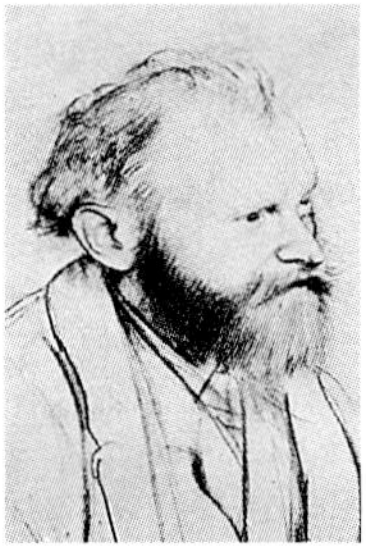

Edouard Manet

■ French painter and engraver, born in Paris in 1832.
■ Between 1850 and 1856, Manet worked in the studio of Thomas Couture, where he acquired his basic mastery. A friend of Baudelaire, Mallarmé and all the great innovators of his time, Manet only occasionally exhibited his work at the Salon; in 1863, his *Luncheon on the Grass* was the key painting at the Salon des Refusés. At the official Salon two years later, his *Olympia* caused a sensation when the emperor himself declared that he was shocked by it.
■ Manet became the idol of a group of younger painters, with whom he met at the Café Guerbois. To these he communicated his love of truth and his will to follow his own inclination rather than the norms imposed by others. At the same time he acknowledged the revelation of open-air painting, and by 1874 his palette had begun to lighten and his manner was more relaxed.
■ In his quest for official recognition, he tried renting a pavilion to exhibit his paintings at the 1867 Universal Exposition. This was a failure. He refused, however, to exhibit alongside the Impressionists, preferring to remain at the Official Salon.
■ Manet died in Paris in 1883, after a long illness. In 1899, *Olympia* entered the Musée du Luxembourg and was shortly afterward moved to the Louvre.
■ Always a paradoxical painter, Manet evolved a smooth, taut manner of his own; this became more fluid after he met Monet (*Monet in his floating studio*, 1874). His subjects, like his technique, lie at the source of modern painting, which springs from a rejection of all illusion.

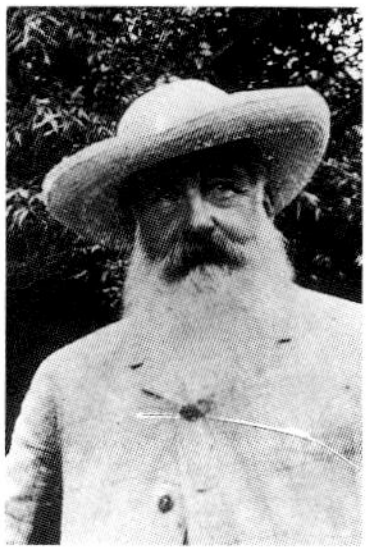

Claude Monet

■ French painter, born in Paris in 1840.
■ As a teenager, Monet acquired a reputation at Le Havre for his caricatures. Encouraged by Boudin, he began painting the Norman coastline; in 1862, he went to Paris, where he communicated his love of open-air work to his new friends Bazille, Renoir, Sisley and Pissarro. Like them, he rejected all instruction and went often to paint outdoors in the Forest of Fontainebleau.
■ During the war of 1870, Monet took refuge in London. On his return to France, he went with his mistress Camille to live at Argenteuil.
■ In 1874, Monet exhibited his *Impression, sunrise*, after which the group of artists showing with him were derisively dubbed "Impressionists". In 1880, he took his work back to the Salon,though he also participated in the seventh Impressionist exhibition in 1882.
■ In the course of redefining the perspectives of Impressionism after 1891, he resorted to the "series" technique, whereby he handled the same subject over and over, with differing atmospheres and light qualities, until it virtually evaporated in paint.
■ After moving to Giverny in 1886, Monet transformed his garden into an infinite mine of subject matter, painting larger and larger pictures of it until his death in 1926.
■ Around 1870, Monet found a style of his own, consisting of rapid cross-hatched brushstrokes which indicated an almost simultaneous transition from sight to canvas. The atmospheric envelope that surrounds things and the luminous continuity in nature were his main concerns. At the end of his life, nearly blind, his brushwork became coarser and his colours deeper and more tortured.

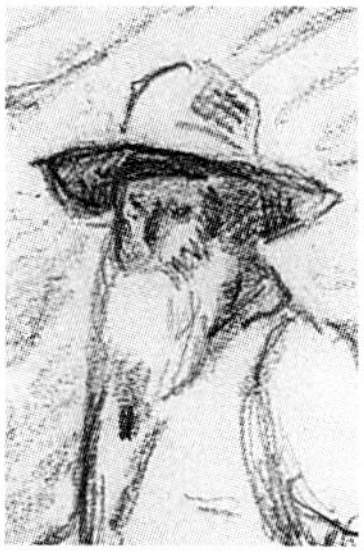

Camille Pissarro

■ French/Danish painter, born at St Thomas (Danish Antilles) in 1830.
■ In his youth, Pissarro worked as a trader. In 1855, he decided to devote himself to painting and moved to Paris, where he fell under Corot's influence, painted from life, and attended the Académie Suisse. Here he met Monet and Cézanne. Nearly all of the work he did prior to 1870 was destroyed during the Franco-Prussian war.
■ Until the last ten years of his life, Pissarro was in constant financial straits; he sold few pictures and had to support a large family. This necessitated moving outside Paris, first to Louveciennes and then to Pontoise.
■ Pissarro took part in the first Impressionist Exhibition 1874, and thereafter was the only artist represented at every one of the others.
■ Politically, Pissarro was an anarchist, who sought a way to communicate in his paintings his concept of life. He unhesitatingly embraced the greatest innovations, notably those of Cézanne and Seurat.
■ When he died in Paris in 1903, his generosity and artistic courage were acknowledged by all.
■ After coming under the influence of the Barbizon School and Courbet, around 1870 Pissarro adopted a more nervous painting manner. His brushwork was thick and crusted, the materials he used had the intended effect of breaking nature up into small units, equivalent and harmonious. In 1886-1890, he adopted (though not systematically) Seurat's principles of "divisionism". As a painter of nature transformed by man's activities, Pissarro was especially successful at rendering the feverish energy of the modern city.

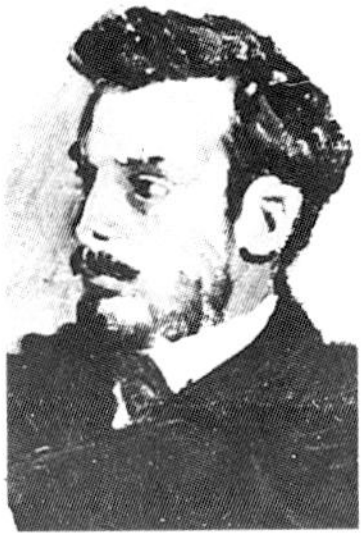

Pierre-Auguste Renoir

■ French painter, born Limoges 1841.
■ Renoir's father was a tailor, and he himself served his apprenticeship as a painter on porcelain. Throughout his life, he retained craftsmanship as his model of artistic probity. He entered Gleyre's studio in 1861 and began showing his paintings at the Salon, with considerable success, in 1864.
■ Bazille, Monet and Sisley converted Renoir to open-air painting, with a freer manner and a livelier palette than he had used hitherto. He took part in the first three Impressionist exhibitions before deciding to return to the Salon in 1878, distancing himself from the group. Nevertheless his friendship with Monet and Cézanne was unaffected.
■ A painter of simple pleasures in central and suburban Paris (*Boaters' Picnic*, 1880), Renoir was also an accomplished society portraitist (*Portrait of Mme Charpentier and her children*, 1879). His links with the other Impressionists were confirmed by his role as Caillebotte's executor.
In 1884, he suggested the forming of a new artistic association, the "Société des Irrégularistes". He showed himself an unorthodox disciple of Ingres with his early *Bathers*, before turning to a softer, more unctuous style, with generously-proportioned models in the image of his wife Aline Charigot.
■ In quest of an all-absorbant quality of light, he moved to the South of France at the turn of the century. He died at Cagnes-sur-Mer in 1919, laden with honours; his eldest son Jean went on to become one of France's most brilliant filmakers.

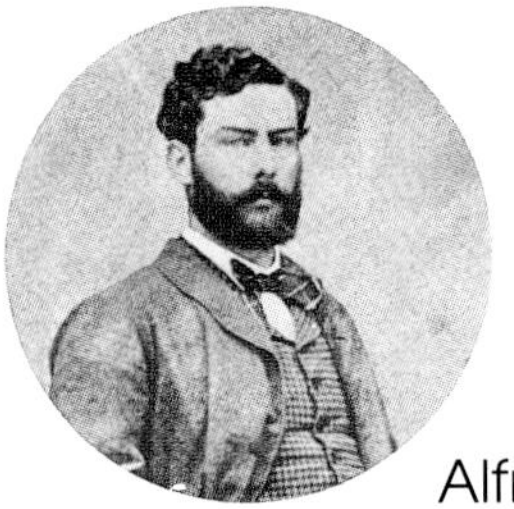

Alfred Sisley

■ English painter, born in Paris in 1839.
■ Sisley's family intended that he should become a businessman; but he took advantage of his visit to London in 1855 to embark on a career as a painter. Back in Paris, he attended Gleyre's studio, where he worked alongside Bazille, Monet and Renoir. In 1870, the Franco-Prussian War ruined his father and obliged Sisley to support his wife Eugènie and their son entirely alone. After escaping to London, he returned to France in 1871 and established himself near Marly-le-Roi.
■ Like Renoir, Sisley participated in the first three Impressionist exhibitions, before deciding to return to the Salon. His paintings were only moderately successful, and it was not until a year after his death that they began to fetch enormous prices.
■ In order to live in relative comfort on the extremely modest means available to him, Sisley spent the closing years of his life in isolation at Moret-sur-Loing, where he died, poor and sick, in 1899.
■ Sisley's work was characterized by his fidelity to a few chosen sites–the outskirts of London, Marly and Moret–and by a determination to work from life and render the specific light of certain places at certain hours.

Maps* of important Impressionist sites

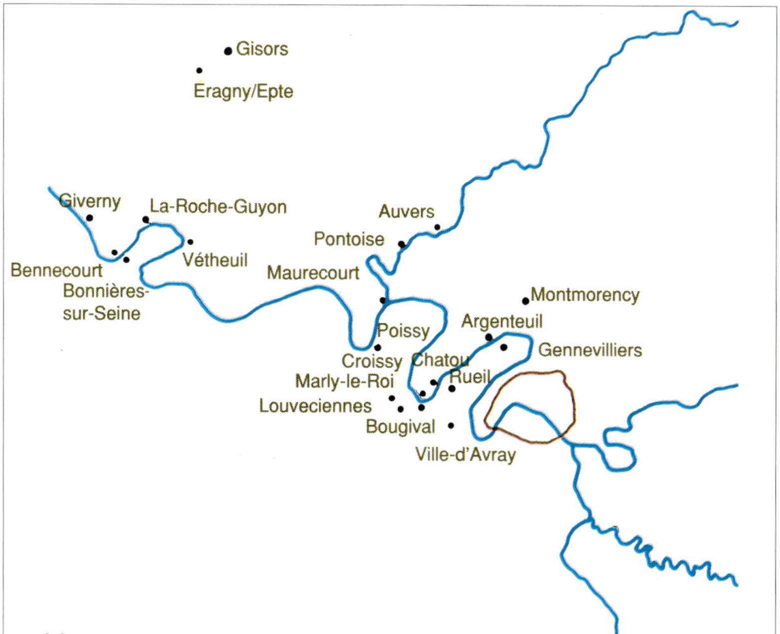

MAP OF THE WEST OF PARIS

Painter and place

— Argenteuil: Monet 1871–1878, Manet 1874, Renoir 1873–1882 and 1888, Caillebotte 1885, Sisley 1872
— Auvers-sur-Oise: Renoir, Pissarro, and Monet, Cézanne 1872–1873 and 1879–1882
— Bennecourt: Monet 1868, Cézanne 1866
— Bonnières-sur-Seine: Cézanne 1866
— Bougival: Monet and Renoir 1869, Morisot 1881–1883, Pissarro 1872, Sisley 1872–1873
— Chatou: Renoir 1879–1881
— Croissy-sur-Seine: Renoir and Monet 1869
— Eragny-sur-Epte: Pissarro 1884–1892
— Gennevilliers: Manet around 1874, Morisot 1875, Caillebotte 1880 –1894
— Gisors: Pissarro 1884–1885
— Giverny: Monet 1883–1926
— La Roche-Guyon: Pissaro 1857, Renoir 1885–1886
— Le Chou: Morisot 1863
— Le Mesnil: Cassatt 1894–1926
— Louveciennes: Pissarro 1869–1870, 1871–1872, Monet 1869, Sisley 1869–1878, Renoir 1869
— Marly-le-Roi: Sisley 1868–1875, Cassatt 1880
— Maurecourt: Morisot 1872–1874
— Mézy : Morisot 1890–1891
— Montmorency: Pissarro 1857–1859
— Osny: Pissarro 1883
— Poissy: Monet 1881
— Pontoise: Pissarro 1866–1868, then 1872–1883, Cézanne 1872–1873 and 1877–1882
— Rueil: Manet 1882
— Vétheuil: Monet 1878–1881
— Ville-d'Avray: Morisot 1861–1863, Monet 1866–1867, Renoir 1868
— Villeneuve-la-Garenne: Sisley 1872, Morisot 1875

* To make the maps easier to read, only the best-known sites are shown.

Painter and place

North of the Loire:

— Barbizon: Sisley 1861
— Belle-Ile-en-Mer: Monet 1886
— Berck-sur-Mer: Manet 1873, Renoir and Sisley 1866
— Boulogne-sur-Mer: Manet 1864–1872, Degas 1869
— Chailly-en-Bière: Sisley 1864, Monet 1863–1865, Bazille 1863–1865, Renoir 1863–1865, Pissarro 1864
— Cherbourg: Manet 1864
— Diénay (Is-sur-Tille): Degas 1890
— Dieppe: Monet 1882, Sisley, Pissarro 1900–1902, Degas 1885, Renoir 1879
— Essoyes (Aube): Renoir from 1886 to 1919
— Étretat: Degas 1869, Monet 1885–1886
— Honfleur: Monet 1858–1867, Bazille 1864
— La Varenne-St-Hilaire: Pissarro 1863–1865 (on the banks of the Marne)
— Le Havre: Monet 1858–1873, Bazille 1864, Sisley, Pissarro 1903
— Le Ménil-Hubert (Orne): Degas 1861
— Lorient: Morisot 1869
— Maincy (near Melun): Cézanne 1879–1880
— Marlotte: Bazille and Sisley 1865–1866, Renoir 1865–1871
— Montfoucault (near Melleray, Sarthe): Pissarro 1874–1876
— Montgeron: Manet 1876, Monet 1877
— Moret-sur-Loing: Sisley 1882–1899
— Pont-Aven: Morisot 1866, Renoir 1892–95
— Pornic: Renoir 1892
— Portrieux: Monet 1894
— Rouen: Bazille, Renoir, Sisley 1894, Monet 1872 and 1892–1893, Pissarro 1883, 1888 and 1895–1898
— Saint-Briac: Renoir 1878
— Saint-Valéry-sur-Somme: Degas 1857 and 1895
— Trouville: Manet 1867, Degas 1869, Monet 1870, Caillebotte 1880–1884, Morisot 1864
— Varangeville-sur-Pourville: Monet 1882 and 1897
— Veneux-Nadon: Sisley 1880–1882
— Villers-sur-Mer: Degas 1869
— Wargemont (near Dieppe): Renoir 1879–1885
— Yerres: Caillebotte 1876–1878

South of the Loire:

— Aix-en-Provence: Cézanne 1839–1906, Monet 1883, Renoir 1883–1901
— Antibes: Monet 1888
— Arcachon: Manet 1871
— Beaulieu-sur-Mer: Renoir 1893
— Bordeaux: Manet 1871
— Cagnes-sur-Mer: Renoir 1895–1919
— Fresselines (Creuse): Monet 1889
— Hyères: Renoir and Monet 1883
— L'Estaque: Cézanne 1869–1871, 1876–1879, 1882–1885, Renoir 1882
— Le Cannet: Renoir 1900–1903
— Le Lavandou: Renoir 1891
— Les Martigues: Renoir 1888
— Magagnosc: Renoir 1900
— Menton: Monet and Renoir 1883–1884
— Méric, near Montpellier: Bazille 1867–1870
— Nice: Renoir 1912–1919, Morisot 1881 and 1888
— Saint-Raphaël: Renoir 1883
— Tamaris: Renoir 1891

Abroad (not on maps):

— Algeria: Renoir 1881–1882
— Italy: Manet 1853, Degas 1856–1860, Renoir 1881–1882
— London: Pissarro 1870–1871, 1890, 1892, 1897
— United States: Degas 1872–1873

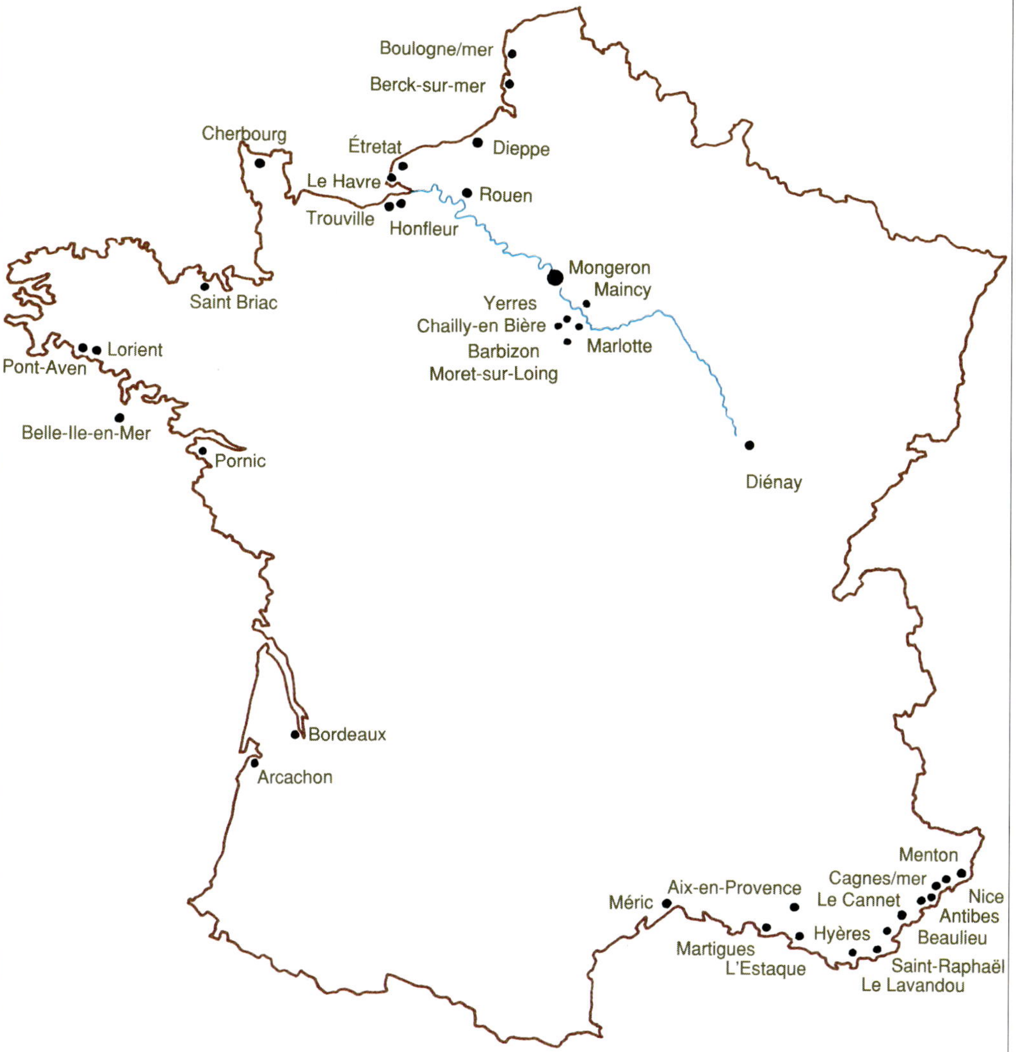

Map of France

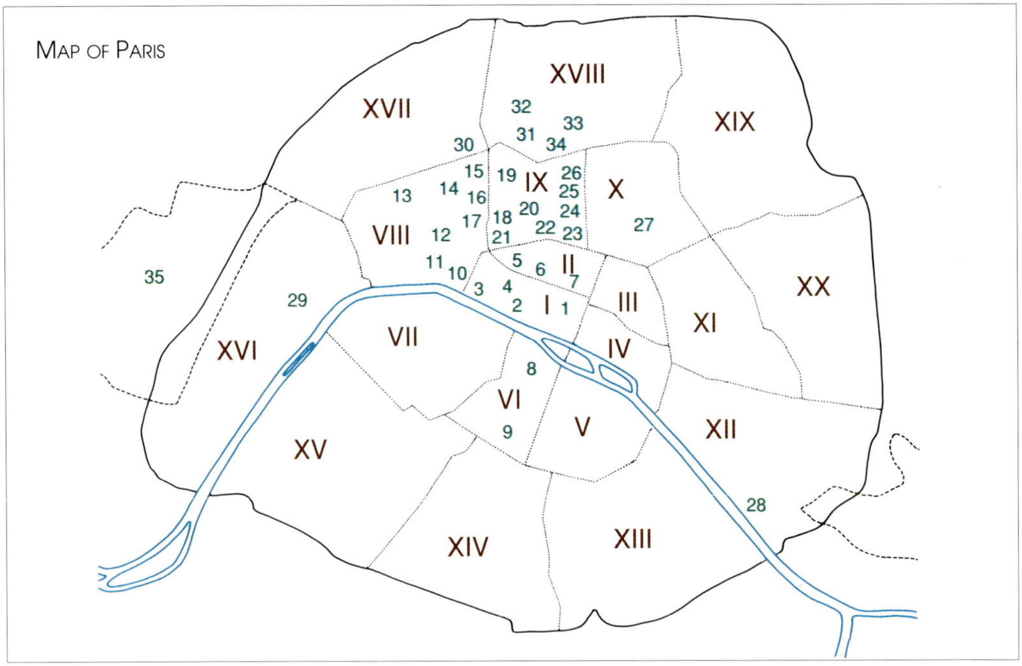

Schools:

— Atelier Gleyre, rue de l'Ouest (XIVe): Monet, Bazille, Sisley and Renoir
— Ecole des Beaux-Arts, quai Malaquais (VIe): Manet, Renoir, Degas
— Académie Suisse, quai des Orfèvres (Ier): Manet, Monet, Pissarro, Cézanne

Cafés:

— Brasserie des Martyrs, 75 rue des Martyrs (IXe): Pissarro and Monet
— Café Guerbois, 9 avenue de Clichy (XVIIIe) (ex Grand-rue-des Batignolles): Manet 1866–1874 with Bazille, Monet, Renoir, Sisley, Pissarro and Cézanne
— La Nouvelle Athènes, place Pigalle (IXe): Manet and group approx. 1876–1886
— Café Tortoni, boulevard des Italiens (IXe): Manet
— Café de Bade: 32 boulevard des Italiens (IXe): Manet
— Maison Dorée, boulevard des Italiens (IXe): Manet
— Brasserie Reischshoffen, boulevard de Rochechouart (IXe): Manet around 1879
— Café La Rochefoucauld (today La Joconde), rue Notre-Dame-de-Lorette (IXe): Degas' favourite café

Homes and studios:

— Studios of Bazille
- 6 rue Furstenberg (VIe), until 1866 (with Monet)
- 20 rue Visconti (VIe), 1867 (with Monet and Renoir)
- 9 rue de la Condamine (XVIIe), 1868–1870 (with Renoir)

— Caillebotte's residences
- 77 rue de Mirosmenil (XVIIIe), 1867–1878
- 31 blvd Haussmann (IXe), after 1878

— Cassatt's studio and apartment
- 10 rue Marignan (VIIIe), after 1887

— Homes and studios of Cézanne
- Rue Coquillière (Ier), 1861
- Rue des Feuillantines (V^{e}), 1861
- 22 rue Beautreillis (IVe), 1865–1867
- 53 rue Notre-Dame-des-Champs (VIe), 1870
- 5 rue de Chevreuse (VIe), 1871

- 4 rue de Jussieu (V^e^), 1871
- Villa des Arts (XVIIIe), at the end of his life

— Degas' apartments and studios
- 4 rue Mondovi (Ier), 1853–1859
- 13 rue de Laval (IXe), 1859–1872
- 77 rue Blanche (IXe), 1872–1876
- 4 rue Frochot (IXe), 1876–1877
- 50 rue Lepic (XIe), 1877–1882
- 21 rue Pigalle (IXe), 1882–1890
- 37 rue Victor-Massé (IXe), 1890–1912
- 6 blvd de Clichy (XVIIIe), 1912–1917

— Manet's studios and apartments
- Rue Lavoisier (VIIIe), 1856–1859
- Rue de la Victoire (IXe), 1859–1860
- Rue de Douai (IXe), 1860
- Rue Médéric (XVIIe), 1861-1870
- 34 blvd des Batignolles (XVIIe), 1864–1867
- 49 rue de St-Petersbourg (XVIIIe), 1867–1878
- 51 rue de St-Petersbourg (XVIIIe), 1870–1872
- 4 rue de St-Petersbourg (XVIIIe), 1870–1872
- 77 rue d'Amsterdam (IXe), 1879–1883
- 39 rue de St-Petersbourg (XVIIIe), 1879–1883

— Monet's homes and studios
- 17 rue de Moncey (IXe), 1862
- 8 rue d'Isly (VIIIe), 1871
- 26 rue d'Edimbourg (VIIIe), 1878

— Morisot's homes and studios
- Rue Franklin (XVIe), 1864–1874
- Rue de Villejust, 1883–1885

— Pissarro's homes and studios
- 16 and 46 rue Notre-Dame-de-Lorette (IXe), 1856
- 38 bis rue Fontaine-St-Georges (IXe), 1858
- 39 rue de Douai (IXe), 1860
- 57 rue de Vanves (XIVe), 1864
- 108 blvd de Rochechouart (XVIIIe), 1866–1868
- 18 rue des Trois-Frères (XVIIIe), 1878–1883

— Renoir's homes and studios
- 23 rue d'Argenteuil (Ier), 1855–1868
- 34 rue Notre-Dame-des-Champs (VIe), 1871–1873
- 35 rue St-Georges (IXe), 1873–1882
- 12 rue Cortot (XVIIIe), 1876
- 6 allée des Brouillards (XVIIIe), 1890–1894
- 73 rue Caulaincourt (XVIIIe), 1901–1904

— Sisley's studio
- 27 cité des Fleurs (XVIIe), 1870–1879

Paris: places portrayed:
(numbered according to the area)

1— Rue Saint-Denis: Monet (1878)
2— Musée du Louvre: Monet (1867), Degas
3— Jardin des Tuileries: Monet (1876), Renoir (1875), Manet (1862), Pissarro (1899–1900)
4— Avenue de l'Opéra: Pissarro (1897–1899)
5— Blvd des Italiens: Pissarro
6— Palais Brogniard (Bourse): Degas (1879)
7— Rue Montorgeuil: Monet (1878)
8— Quai du Louvre, Quai Voltaire, and the Pont-Neuf: Monet (1867–1872), Renoir (1867–1872), Pissarro (1898–1903)
9— Jardin du Luxembourg: Caillebotte (1876)
10— Place de la Concorde: Monet (1875)
11— Les Ambassadeurs, Champs-Elysées (the present Espace Cardin): Manet and Degas (1875–1878)
12— Blvd Haussmann: Caillebotte (1880)
13— Parc Monceau: Monet (1876–1877), Caillebotte (1876–1877)
14— Pont de l'Europe: Caillebotte (1876–1877), Manet (1873), Monet (1877)
15— Rue Mosnier, rue de Berne: Manet (1879)
16— Crossroad, rue de Turin: Caillebotte (1877)
17— Gare St-Lazare: Monet (1875–1877)
18— Place du Havre and rue St-Lazare: Pissarro (1893, 1897)
19— Rue d'Amsterdam: Pissarro
20— Opéra, Palais Garnier: Degas (1876 until at least 1883), Renoir (1874–1880), Cassatt (1879–1882)
21— Blvd des Capucines: Monet (1873–1874)
22— Rue Halévy: Caillebotte (1878)
23— Blvd Montmartre: Pissarro (1897)
24— Opéra, rue Le-Peletier: Manet (1873) and Degas (1868–73)
25— Les Folies-Bergères, rue Richer: Manet (1881–1882)
26— Cirque Fernando, boulevard de Rochechouart: Manet, Degas (1879) and Renoir
27— Canal St-Martin: Sisley (1870)
28— Quai de Bercy: Cézanne (1872)
29— Trocadéro: Morisot (1866–1872), Manet (1867)
30— Le Père Lathuille (at the Batignolles): Manet (1879)
31— Moulin de la Galette, 81 rue Lepic: Renoir (1876) and Cézanne
32— Rue des Saules (Montmartre): Cézanne (1867)
33— Montmartre: Sisley (1869)
34— Blvd de Rochechouart: Pissarro (1878)
35— Bois de Boulogne: Renoir (1868–1873), Morisot (1879–1884), Cassatt (1881), Degas (at Longchamp, 1866–1885), Manet (1864–1872)

Chronological references

PAINTINGS SHOWN

1860:
Manet, *Portrait of M. and Mme Auguste Manet*.

1863
Manet, The *Luncheon on the Grass*.
Manet, *Olympia*.
Rousseau, *Woodland Clearing*.

1864:
Boudin, *Beach at Trouville*.
Manet, *Peonies*.

1865–1866:
Monet, *Luncheon on the Grass*.

1858–1867:
Degas, *Family Portrait*.

1867:
Monet, *Terrace at St-Adresse*.
Manet, *View of the Universal Exposition*.
Renoir, *Frédéric Bazille at his Easel*.
Bazille, *Family Reunion*.

1868:
Manet, *Portrait of Emile Zola*.
Manet, *Portrait of Théodore Duret*.

1868–1869:
Manet, *The Balcony*.

THE IMPRESSIONISTS

1863:
Salon des Refusés: Manet's *The Luncheon on the Grass*.
Manet marries Suzanne Leenhoff.

1865:
Manet shows *Olympia* and *Christ* at the Salon: scandal.

1866:
Manet shows *Camille* at the Salon: Cézanne is rejected.

1867:
Manet rents a pavilion to show his work.
Petition for a new "Salon des Refusés".
Bazille, Renoir and Monet work together.

1868:
Berthe Morisot meets Manet and Degas.

1870:
Monet marries Camille Doncieux.
Monet and Pissarro in England: they meet Paul Durand-Ruel.
Bazille is killed at the battle of Beaune-la-Rolande.
Degas, Manet and Renoir join the National Guard.
Cézanne at l'Estaque.

ARTISTIC LIFE IN PARIS

1855
Universal Exposition on the Champs-Elysées: Courbet displays his paintings in the "Pavillon du Réalisme".

1857:
Baudelaire publishes *Les Fleurs du Mal*; Flaubert publishes *Madame Bovary*.

1859:
A decree gives sweeping powers to the Prefect of the Seine department, Haussmann, who transforms Paris by creating new boulevards.

1863:
Death of Delacroix.
Caganel's *Birth of Venus* is a huge success at the official Salon.
The Ecole des Beaux-Arts is reformed.

1865:
The Goncourt brothers publish their realist novel, *Germinie Lacerteux*.

1867:
The Universal Exhibition is held in Paris.
Marx publishes volume I of *Das Kapital*.
Deaths of Ingres and Baudelaire.

HISTORICAL EVENTS

1852:
Napoleon III becomes Emperor of France.

1855:
Opening of the Paris-Lyon-Marseilles railway.

1859:
Italian campaign: the French army assists with the unification of Italy.

1861:
American Civil War.

1864:
Maximilian of Austria becomes Emperor of Mexico, supported by the French Army.
Emile Ollivier gives his support to the "liberal" Empire.

1865:
Victory of the Union over the Confederacy in America.
Founding of the Communist International in Paris.

1869:
Bazille, *Summer Scene*.

Bazille, *The Artist's Studio, rue de La Condamine*.

Fantin-Latour, *A Studio in the Batignolles*.

1872:
Morisot, *The Cradle*.

1873:
Monet, *The Luncheon*.
Pissarro, *Portrait of the Artist*.
Degas, *Portrait in an Office*.
Pissarro, *Factory near Pontoise*.
Pissarro, *Hoar-frost*.

1873–1874:
Cézanne, *A Modern Olympia*.

1874:
Renoir, *The Box*.
Monet, *The Railway Bridge, Argenteuil*.
Monet, *Impression, Sunrise*.
Gonzalès, *A Box at the Italiens*.
Cézanne, *The Hanged Man's House*.
Manet, *Claude Monet and his Wife in his Floating Studio*.

1875:
Renoir, *Portrait of Victor Chocquet*.
Monet, *The Coal Heavers*.

1871:
Monet moves to Argenteuil.

1872:
Return of Cassatt to Europe after 2 years' absence.

1873:
Second Salon des Refusés.
Morisot marries Eugène Manet.

1874:
January 13: First Hoschedé sale.
April-May: Opening of the "First Exhibition of the Cooperative Limited Company of artists, painters, sculptors, engravers and lithographers", the first "impressionist" exhibition, at Nadar's house on 35 blvd des Capucines.
Cézanne, Degas, Guillaumin, Monet, Morisot, Pissarro, Renoir, Sisley.
Manet refuses to take part.
Louis Leroy mocks the group as "impressionists".

1875:
March 24: Public auction of "oil paintings and watercolours by Monet, Morisot, Renoir and Sisley".
Impressionist exhibition at Durand-Ruel's in London.

1869:
Inauguration of the Folies-Bergères.

1871:
Completion of Baltard's Eglise Saint-Augustin.
Zola publishes the first volume of his *Rougon-Macquart* series.

1872:
Construction begins on the Fourvière basilica in Lyon.
Jules Verne publishes *Around the World in 80 Days*.

1873:
The Opéra on rue Le Peletier is burne down.
Rimbaud writes *Une Saison en Enfer*.

1875:
Death of Corot.
Inauguration of Garnier's new Opera House.
Construction of the Basilica of Sacré-Coeur at Montmartre begins.

Bizet : *Carmen*

1876:
Mallarmé publishes *L'après-midi d'un faune*.
Michelet publishes *Histoire du XXe siècle*.

1867:
Maximilian is executed in Mexico.

1869:
The Suez Canal opens.

1870:
Franco-Prussian War.
September: Abdication of Napoleon III.

1871:
January: Fondation of the German Empire.
Capitulation of Paris.
February: Formation of Thiers' government.
March: Proclamation of the Paris commune, which is crushed in June after bitter fighting.

1873:
End of the German occupation of France.
Fall of Thiers; Marshal Mac-Mahon becomes President of the Republic.
September: Abortive attempt to restore the monarchy.
November: *Loi du Septennat*.
Financial crisis.

1874
May: Fall of de Broglie's conservative government.

1875:
Caillebotte, *The Floor Planers*.

Renoir, *Study, Torso, Effect of Sunshine*.

1873–1876:
Degas, *Dance Class*.

1875–1876:
Degas, *At the Café*.

1876:
Monet, *The Tuileries*.

Manet, *Portrait of Stéphane Mallarmé*.

Renoir, *Bal du Moulin de la Galette*.
Degas, *Robert le Diable's ballet*.
Sisley, *Floods at Port-Marly*.

1876–1877:
Degas, *Ballet*.

1877:
Monet, *The Pont de l'Europe, Gare Saint-Lazare*.
Pissarro, *Red Roofs, corner of a village, effect of winter*.

1878–1879:
Cézanne, *L'Estaque*.

1879:
Degas, *Portraits of Friends on Stage*.

1860–1880:
Degas, *Spartan Girls Taunting Youths*

1876:
Manet invites the public to view his canvases in his studio, after another rejection by the Salon.
April: Second Exhibition at the Durand-Ruel gallery, rue Le Peletier: Caillebotte participates but not Cézanne. Durant publishes *La nouvelle peinture*, in which he defends the group and especially Degas.

1877:
April: Third Impressionist Exhibition: Caillebotte, Cézanne, Degas, Guillaumin, Manet, Morisot, Pissarro, Renoir, Sisley. Degas wins his point, that the exhibition should not be called "Impressionist". While the exhibition lasts, Georges Rivière (assisted by Chocquet) publishes a review called *L'Impressionniste*.

1878:
Renoir shows *The Cup of Chocolate* at the Salon.
Duret publishes *Les Peintres Impressionnistes*.

1879:
Manet's *Execution of Emperor Maximilian* is shown in the USA.
Fourth exhibition of "Independent Realist and Impressionist artists", without Cézanne, Monet, Renoir and Sisley. Cassatt and Forain take part.

1877:
Rodin's sculpture the *Age of Bronze* is shown at the Salon: he is accused of moulding it straight from a living body.
Saint-Saëns composes *Samson et Dalila*.

1878:
Universal Exposition, Paris.
Muybridge breaks down the motion of a horse with photographs.

1879:
Death of Thomas Couture.

1880:
The state ceases to organize the official Salon.
Maupassant publishes *Boule de Suif*.
Rodin exhibits *Le Penseur*.
Taine publishes *La philosophie de l'Art*.

1875:
Wallon Amendment: France is a Republic.

1876:
Political crisis after the Republican victory at the legislative elections.

1877:
Gambetta's speech against clericalism. Mac-Mahon names the Prince de Broglie President du Conseil and dissolves the Assembly.
Fresh Republican victory and collapse of the monarchist cause.
Death of Thiers.

1879:
Mac-Mahon resigns.
Jules Grévy elected President: the Republicans in control.

Chambres returns to Paris.

Pasteur discovers the anti-rabies vaccine.

1880:
Manet, *Asparagus*.
Cassatt, *Autumn*.

1879–1880:
Degas, *14-year-old Ballerina*.

1880–1881:
Manet, *Rochefort's Escape*.

1881:
Renoir, *The Railway Bridge at Chatou*.
Renoir, *The Mosque*.

1879–1882:
Cézanne, *Apples and Biscuits*.
Cézanne, *Bathers (Les Grandes Baigneuses)*.

1884:
Degas, *Women Ironing*, *around*.

1885:
Seurat, *Field of Lucerne at Saint-Denis*.

1876–1887:
Degas, *At the Races: Amateur Jockeys*.

1886–1888:
Pissarro, *View from my Window, Eragny-sur-Epte*.

1887:
Bazille, *Portrait of Auguste Renoir*.

1889 :
Caillebotte, *Self-portrait*.

1885–1890:
Cézanne, *Portrait of Madame Cézanne*.

Renoir is successful at the Salon.
Camille Manet dies.

1880:
Fifth Exhibition: Cézanne, Monet, Renoir and Sisley are absent. Gauguin participates.
Monet has a one-man show at La Vie Moderne.

1881:
Sixth Exhibition, dominated by Degas. Even Caillebotte is absent.

1882:
Seventh Exhibition of "independents" at the Durand-Ruel Gallery, rue Saint-Honoré: Caillebotte, Gauguin, Guillaumin, Monet, Morisot, Pissarro, Renoir, Sisley. Degas and Cassatt are notable absentees.
The stock market failure brings Durand-Ruel to the brink of bankruptcy.
Cézanne is admitted to the Salon for the first time.

1883:
Death of Manet.

1885:
Monet takes part in the International Exhibition at Georges Petit's: disagreements with Durand-Ruel.

1881:
Courbet's *Burial at Ornans* enters the Musée du Luxembourg.

1882:
Creation of the Union Centrale des Arts Décoratifs.

1883:
Fauré's *Requiem* performed.

1884:
Seurat founds the Salon des Independants, without juries or prizes.

1885:
Victor Hugo's state funeral.
Nietzsche publishes *Thus Spoke Zarathustra*.

1880:
Decree banning unauthorized religious meetings.
Expulsion of the Jesuits.

1881–1882:
Gambetta's ministry.

1882:
Collapse of the Union Générale: financial crisis.
The Loi Jules Ferry (lay schools and compulsory education) is passed.

1884:
Trades Unions are made legal.
Divorce law passed.

1886:
Bloody repression of the Decazeville strike.

1887:
Wilson scandal: Grévy, accused of corruption, resigns.

1890–1891:
Guillaumin, *Paris Suburbs*.
Cassatt, *The Bath*.

1891:
Monet, *Haystacks*.

1890–1892:
Degas, *Landscape*.

1892:
Renoir, *Girls at the Piano*.

Monet, *Rouen Cathedral. Effect of sunlight. End of the day.*

1893:
Morisot, *Julie Manet and her dog Laërte*.

1890–1894:
Cézanne, *La Montagne Sainte-Victoire*.

1894:
Monet, *Rouen Cathedral : harmony in blue and gold full sunshine*.

1895:
Degas, *Woman Bathing*.

1895–1898:
Degas, *After the Bath*.

1896–1898:
Degas, *Injured Jockey*.

1898:
Pissarro, *Avenue de l'Opéra*.

1898:
Pissarro, *Place du Théâtre-Français*.

1886:
Pissarro meets Seurat and Signac, who convert him to "neo-Impressionism". Eight and last Impressionist Exhibition: Cassatt, Degas, Forain, Gauguin, Guillaumin, Morisot. The Divisionists are represented by Pissarro, Seurat and Signac.
Impressionist exhibition in New York organized by Durand-Ruel. Fénélon publishes *Les Impressionistes* in 1886.

1889:
Pissarro invites Van Gogh to stay.

1890:
National subscription to buy Manet's *Olympia*.

1894:
The state accepts part of the Caillebotte bequest.

1895:
Death of Morisot.

1897:
Degas falls out with Pissarro and Halévy over the Dreyfus affair.
Monet and Pissarro support Zola.

1899:
Death of Sisley.

1886:
Gauguin at Pont-Aven.

1887:
Formation of the Nabi group around Sérusier and Maurice Denis.

1889:
Universal Exposition, Paris: Construction of the Eiffel Tower. Suicide of Van Gogh.

1891:
Gauguin's first voyage to Tahiti.

1894:
Durkheim publishes *Les règles de la méthode sociologique*.
Debussy composes *Prélude à l'aprés-midi d'un faune*.

1895:
Discovery of the X-Ray.
First cinema projection by the Lumière brothers.

1897:
Barrès publishes *Les Déracinés*.

1889:
Boulanger crisis, exile of General Boulanger.
Founding of 2nd Socialist International.

1891:
Papal encyclical *Rerum Novarum*.
The Catholics acknowledge the Republic.

1894:
Assassination of President Carnot: "lois scélérates" voted, to suppress anarchism.
Beginning of the Dreyfus Affair.

1898:
Zola publishes "J'accuse" in *L'Aurore*, Clémenceau's newspaper,
demanding the rehabilitation of Dreyfus. Anti-Semites and intellectuals violently polarized.

1895–1899:
Cézanne, *Red Rock* and *Portrait of Ambroise Vollard*.

1895–1900:
Cézanne, *Still life with Onions*.

1903:
Pissarro, *Pont-Royal* and *Pavillon de Flore*.

1900–1906:
Cézanne, *Bathers* and *Black Castle*.

1909:
Renoir, *The Clown*.

1905–1910:
Degas, *At the Dressmaker's*.

1913:
Vallotton, *Black and White*.

1918–1919:
Renoir, *Bathers*.

1920–1922:
Monet, *Allée des Rosiers, Giverny*.

1916–1923:
Monet, *Waterlilies*.

1959:
Stella, *Plum Island*.

1899:
Sale of the Chocquet collection.
Cézanne exhibits at the Salon des Indépendants.

1900 :
Renoir receives the Légion d'Honneur.

1901:
Maurice Denis exhibits *Hommage à Cézanne* at the Salon des Indépendants.

1903:
Death of Pissarro.

1906:
Death of Cézanne.
Moreau-Nélaton Donation.
Cézanne retrospective at the Salon d'Automne.

1912:
Renoir undergoes a serious operation.

1916:
Death of Degas.

1919:
Death of Renoir.

1922:
Death of Durand-Ruel.

1926:
Death of Cassatt.
Death of Monet.

1900:
Universal Exposition in Paris.

1902:
André Gide publishes *The Immoralist*.

1903:
Foundation of the Salon d'Automne.
First Tour de France.

1905:
"Salle fauve" at the Salon d'Automne, around Matisse.
Einstein formulates his theory of relativity.

Creation of "Die Brücke" in Germany.

1907:
Picasso paints his *Demoiselles d'Avignon*.

1909:
Blériot crosses the Channel in an aeroplane.
Diaghilev's ballet Russe at the Châtelet.

1911:
"Salle cubiste" at the Salon des Indépendants.

1912:
Paul Claudel publishers *L'Annonce faite à Marie*.

1899:
Waldeck-Rousseau ministry, radical and socialist successes (Jaurès).

1900:
Opening of the first Paris Metro line.

1900–1901:
Violent labour strikes.
First issue of *L'Humanité*.

1905:
Separation of church and state.
Foundation of the SFIO.

1906:
Clémenceau's Ministry.

1912:
Paul Deschanel is elected President of the Republic.

1913:
Poincaré becomes President of the Republic.

1914–1918:
First World War.

Glossary

Academies
Studios grouped around a professor, where young artists could study painting and draw from live models, (by-passing the official art-school system of the Ecole Nationale des Beaux-Arts). In the mid-19th century, the most famous academies in Paris were the Académies Julian and Suisse.

Academicism
Tendency to adhere blindly to the aesthetic principles codified by the Académie des Beaux-Arts in the 17th century. Academicism in the 19th century dominated the official teaching of art and the choices of paintings made by the salons.

Art critic
A writer or jounalist who judges works of art. Art critics have always existed, but the literary branch of the profession largely evolved in the 19th century, when newspapers began hiring writers specifically for the task.

Belle Epoque
A period of stability in the French Republic, which lasted from the 1880's till 1914. These years began to be called La Belle Epoque during the First World War.

Brushwork
The traces of the brush on the surface, which gives the painting its individual aspect. With the Impressionists, brushwork became more and more apparent, to the point where each stroke is often independently visible.

Centring
The selection of a vantage point for a painting, and the delimiting of the composition's outer limits. Previously an unimportant feature, centring became a key issue for the Impressionists, who went so far as to truncate their figures on the edges of their canvases.

Chromatics
Manner of using colour (the word is derived from the Greek chromos, colour).

Collector
Private individual who buys or otherwise acquires a work of art. In the late 19th century the importance of the collector was all the greater for artists who were ignored by the official insititutions.

Conventions
Rules and principles which artists had to obey if they wished to conform to official criteria of quality, according to which their work would be selected for the salons.

Commissioning
The practice of paying an artist to create a work of art. In the 19th century, the development of the art market, in which works already created could be sold, removed this constraint.

Composition
The placement of the components of the subject of a painting, i.e. the figures, objects and colours.

Contours
Lines drawn or painted around objects represented on canvas or paper to distinguish them from the things surrounding them.

Dealer
Intermediary between the creator of the art object and his buyer, who purchases the object from the artist and sells it to the collector. Dealers were crucial to the spread of Impressionism, at a time

Dégradé
Progressive lightening of a colour by the addition of a growing quantity of white.

Drawing
The action of placing lines on the surface of canvas or paper. The opposite of colour in the theory of art that emerged from the Renaissance, drawing became less and less differentiated from it in the work of artists who, like Manet, used touches of bright colour to the virtual exclusion of all else.

Engraving
See "print".

Flat Tint
Way of laying on colour as level as possible, without nuances of tone or apparent manipulation of the brush.

Format
The dimensions of a work of art. Quite apart from the equivalent effect produced by reproduction in a book, one must take account of the real format of a given work if one is to grasp its true importance.

Fragment
A part of an object or figure which has been separated from the ensemble to which it naturally belongs. With their way of centring their pictures, the Impressionists tended to fragment nature.

Frame
Wooden battens running round the sides of the canvas to isolate it from the wall and surroundings. Traditionally gilded since the 18th century, the frame also lent value to the picture by giving it the aspect of something precious. The Impressionists were the first to insist that frames be painted white, to make it easier for people to concentrate on the picture and strengthen the impact of its colours.

Genres
Categories of artistic themes. The Académie Française organized a hierarchy of genres which downgraded landscape and installed history painting, usually on antique or mythological themes, at the summit of art. The Impressionists rejected this hierarchy, as well as the distinction between genres.

Harmony
Musical term describing the accord of all the elements in a composition. Also applicable to the plastic arts.

Illusionism
"Illusionism" in painting consists in using all necessary means to make observers believe that whatever is featured on the canvas really exists, and is not merely the creation of an artist. Geometrical perspective (which suggest depth despite the flat surface of the canvas) and an impersonal painting manner (which denies the presence of a painter) have been the principal tools of pictural illusionism since the Renaissance.

Law
When he paints a picture, an artist may respect three kinds of law, which often come into conflict: the laws imposed by an official institution which proscribes certain subjects; the laws of exterior reality; and the laws imposed by the painting itself, which force the artist to paint on a flat surface with a given material.

Low-angle
A cinematic term describing a very low view point, as if the scene were witnessed from below. Now used to describe the same effect in painting, as introduced by the Impressionists.

Manner
An artist's individual way of applying paint; each painter has his own manner, characterized by his paint thickness, the direction of his brushwork, etc.

Materials
That which serves to create a work of art. In their paintings, the Impressionists mainly used oil paints (with pigments liquefied and rendered useable by admixture with oil) but they also blended these with other materials such as gouache, pastel, charcoal, etc. Cézanne and Degas went even further, giving the fabric of their canvases a prominent role in their work.

Model
Person who poses for a painting or sculpture, voluntarily or otherwise. Professional models-sometimes male, more often female.

Monotype
Print technique whereby a metal surface is covered with ink or coloured paint. The image obtained in this way is then printed on paper in one edition only, since it cannot be reproduced identically. Degas was a master of this technique.

Motif
Shape repeated over and over on a surface to give it a decorative aspect. In the vocabulary of the Impressionists, the "motif" designated the place which the artist had to paint by going there himself and doing the work from life, on the spot.

Naturalism
An artistic trend of the mid-19th century, which reached its zenith with Courbet's "realism". Naturalism sought to render an immediate pictural transposition of nature as observed by the human eye.

Object
An ambiguous term which can be used to describe both the things that exist in the real world, and those transcribed by an artist. The object in a painting should not be confused with its subject matter (for example a painting of a landscape may include a landscape as an object, but the harmony of nature as its subject).

Open-air-painting
Doctrine which proclaimed the necessity to paint outside, directly from life, without subsequently retouching the canvas in the studio. Adopted in the early 19th century by the Barbizon painters and by Boudin, open-air painting was elevated to a moral obligation by Monet and the Impressionists.

Pastel
Drawing done with sticks of coloured chalk made from powdered colours and ground white chalk mashed into a paste with glue or gum arabic. Degas transformed the art of pastel, which had previously been the exclusive province of 17th-century society portraitists, into a complex technique.

Perspective
The geometrical construction of the pictural space, formalized in the 15th century, which consists in calculating the diminution of the scale of objects and the direction of lines, to give the illusion of depth on a flat surface.The Impressionists called in question the mathematical logic of perspective, favouring spatial forms of division which were closer to the way people observe scenes in real life.

Plane
Two-dimensional surface on which the artist paints or draws. Since the Renaissance, painters

had sought to give the illusion of depth and volume on this surface. With Impressionism, they began to proclaim that a painting is a flat surface and that it is futile to deny this fact.

Plastic
That which has three-dimensional volume, or gives the illusion of having three-dimensional volume.

Pose
Physical position adopted by the model.

Primary Colours
The triad of colours–red, yellow, blue–combinations of which are the base of all other colours.

Print
Image painted on paper, which has previously been drawn or engraved on a support. The procedures most used by the Impressionists were lithography (the printing of a drawing previously rendered on a flat surface, usually stone) and etching (in which the image is etched on a metal plate).

Realism
See "naturalism".

Relief
Procedures which consists in giving the illusion of volume, by shading, on a two-dimensional surface such as canvas or paper.

Salons
Periodical shows organized to allow artists to show their works without having to go through a dealer. In the 19th century, the Official Salon was presided over by a jury dominated by members of the Académie des Beaux-Arts, who selected the works and attributed prizes to them. In 1863, then in 1873, the very large numbers of rejected works prompted the organization of a Salon des Refusés.

Series
The principle of painting a number of versions of the same subject and format, with only the light and colours at variance. Invented and strictly applied by Monet, the series principle was intermittently practiced by the other Impressionists.

Subject
See "object".

Value
Describes the intensity of a colour in relation to light and shadow.

Vanishing point
In perspective, the point, or points, toward which all lines converge, defining the depth of a composition.

View/Vantage Point
The point where the eye of the spectator or artist is theoretically positioned, to look at or paint a picture. The Impressionists often viewed their subject matter from eccentric points of vantage, which allowed them to emphasize the immediacy of their scenes.

Work
Word designating either a unique piece created by an artist, or his life's work.

photographic credits

Arthephot, Paris: pp. 52-photo Roland, 53a-photo Held, 72-photo Held, 84al-photo Hinz
Ashmolean Museum, Oxford: p.67a
Bibliothèque Nationale, Paris: pp. 35a, 38al, 55, 58a, 73b, 75a, 99
BL– Giraudon, Paris: p. 37a
Bridgeman Art Library, London: pp. 9a (Fogg Art Museum Harvard University, Cambridge MA), 38b, 40al, 53b, 58b, 62ar, 67b, 84b
British Museum, London: p. 100b
Éditions Scala , Paris: pp. 12, 13a, 14l, 16ar, 16al, 18b, 18al, 20al, 24al, 27, 31d, 33, 43, 44, 45a, 47b, 49a, 50b, 50a, 56b, 65, 69a, 71, 77, 79b, 81a, 87, 88, 91, 93 , 95, 104, 105
Fogg Art Museum, Harvard University Art Museum, Cambridge MA: p. 30 (gift of Mr & Mrs F. Meynier de Salinelles)
Galerie Jean Krugier, Genève: p. 100a
Giraudon, Paris: p. 89a
Lauros– Giraudon, Paris: p. 75b
Metropolitan Museum of Art, New York: pp. 60d, 94b
Musée des Beaux-Arts, Reims: p.74
Musée Marmottan, Paris: pp. 10-11b, 22a, 70, 73a, 92, 101
Musée national d'Art moderne, Paris: p. 8
Museum of Fine Arts, Springfield MA: p. 68
Öffentliche Kunstsammlung, Bâle: p. 45b-photo Bühler
Photothèque des musées de la Ville de Paris: pp. 20ar, 24b, 32, 62b, 91a
Réunion des Musées nationaux, Paris: pp. 10a, 11a, 14b, 14ar, 16b, 18ar, 20b, 22b, 22ar, 22al, 24ar, 26, 28, 29b, 31l, 34, 35b, 36, 37b, 38al, 40b, 40ar, 41, 46, 47a, 48, 51, 56a, 57, 59, 60b, 60al, 62 al, 64, 66, 69b, 76, 78, 79a, 80, 81b, 82b, 82ar, 82al, 84ar, 86, 89b, 90, 94a, 96, 97l, 97a, 98, 102, 103b, 103a, 106-107
Roger-Viollet, Paris: pp. 6-7, 9b
© Héritiers Matisse, Paris: p. 8
© Jean-Bernard Naudin, Paris: p. 13b
© Spadem, Paris 1995: p.45

Designer: Jérôme Faucheux
Layout by Maxence Scherf
Corrections: Céline Chiflet
Photoengraving: Editoriale, Trieste
Printed by Editoriale, Trieste
Dépôt légal: July 1995